MANAGING SCARCE RESOURCES FOR JAILS

Mark Pogrebin

UNIVERSITY
PRESS OF
AMERICA

To Janet, who always understood.

iv

Acknowledgment

I owe my most profound gratitude to both Sheriff Jack Dolan and Sheriff Michael Ashe, Jr. for opening up their correctional programs for study and making their staff available for interviews.

A special indebtedness is owed to Marie Mactavish, Dr. Paul Katsampes and John Milosovich of the N.I.C. Jail Center in Boulder for their support and assistance for the duration of this project.

Much is owed to Dr. Dail Neugarten of the Graduate School of Public Affairs of the University of Colorado at Denver for her assistance in editing and improving this information package. Finally, I am grateful to Candice Romig and Dolores Michaels for their patience and typing of this book.

Table of Contents

CHAPTER IV   (continued)

List of Figures

List of Tables

INTRODUCTION

Managing Scarce Resources

This country is in an era that has been referred to as one of resource scarcity and organizational decline (Levine, 1979). High inflation, coupled with a national reluctance to increase the tax base results in hard times for government. In carrying out their roles of program managers, fiscal and regulatory agents, personnelists and service providers, public sector managers will be administering cutbacks, tradeoffs, reallocations, organizational contractions, program terminations, and sacrifice (Levine, 1979).

Recent inflation combined with the recent recession has jolted ordinary citizens (Murphy, 1975). Resistance to higher taxes at all levels of government has never been greater, but that resistance, notes Murphy, may be only the tip of the iceberg if economic conditions continue to worsen. This citizen concern is directly reflected in the actions and orientations of elected officials, who have begun to take a much closer look at governmental program objectives and the resources, both allocated and available. The problems of insuring high levels of productivity in the face of greater budgetary constraints is well stated by Levine (1973: 463). He points out that resource scarcity is creating the necessity for governments to terminate some programs, lower the activities of others, and determine tradeoffs between new demands and old programs rather than to expand whenever a public demand arises. The problem confronting administrators is to maintain organizational capacity in the period of resource decline by devising new managerial arrangements, administrative policies and organizational procedures within prevailing structures that were designed during periods of growth. Levine clearly notes the problem for public managers:

> It is a contingency for public employees and clients; employees who must sustain their morale and productivity in the face of increasing control from above and shrinking opportunities for creativity and promotion while clients must find alternative sources for the services governments may no longer be able to provide (463).

xi

Levine (1979) developed the concept "cutback management". According to Levine, "cutback management" is managing organizational change toward lower levels of resource consumption and organizational activity. Cutting back an organization involves making difficult decisions about who will be laid off, which government funded programs will be scaled down or terminated, and what clients will be requested to make sacrifices.

The latter part of the 1970's, notes Miron (1979), saw new pressures for reductions in local government expenditures that would ease the tax burden for citizens. These pressures were the result of:

. . . . inflation as they effect incomes and cost of living on the part of taxpapers, pressures from cyclical recessions, crystallized anti-government malaise on the part of taxpayers, and the success of public or citizen referendum tactics aimed at limiting by law revenue sources or expenditure levels of government (3).

A new form of management in the public sector was the direct effect of taxpayer actions. We are now in an era that is termed cutback management or managing declining resources. Miron (1979) states that taxpayer revolts have resulted in pressures for public officials to reduce or eliminate annual budgetary increments by reducing, limiting or doing away with certain types of revenue producing means (tax reductions), by lowering or eliminating personnel expenditures, or by abolishing certain publically supported programs.

Local governments can no longer project an image of competence; they must be competent. Agency administrators must view this unstable economic period as an opportunity to better understand their relationships with the populations they serve, to analyze their organization's functions and to enact positive reforms in order to manage more effectively those functions which they believe to be essential (May and Meltzer, 1981). Although this appears to be a bleak time for public agency administrators, the potential exists for each organization to get its act together, to make its operations efficient and effective, but more fundamentally, to carve out a domain, an area of responsibility in which services are widely considered to be essential." (Nelson and Harlow, 1980: 66-67)

In their study of the effects of Proposition 13 on California's probation departments, Nelson and Harlow found that responses to cutbacks in probation vary widely. They concluded that there were probation managers who viewed their role as one of support--building in the community as opposed to just responding to scarce resource pressures. These progressive probation administrators exerted pressures of their own. They saw the importance of selling their agencies' mission and goals while at the same time adapting to fiscal constraints. Most important, these managers saw cutbacks as a chance to take advantage of opportunities where they existed. "Our study led us to conclude that, while many California counties were floundering in the wake of Proposition 13, some were using the impetus of fiscal crisis to generate constructive change." (Nelson and Harlow, 1980: 22)

The foregoing concepts are directly applicable to jails which are funded at the county level. These institutions have been affected by budgetary cutbacks at the same time that court orders have required them to provide more services for inmates. Rising costs for ongoing programs will eventually outstrip the availability of funds for new correctional programs and operations. Since the offender will remain a consumer of resources, ways of insuring better returns on resource investment must be found (Richmond, 1972). As is true in other public service areas, there is an increasing demand on the part of the taxpayer for greater accountability from public agencies:

> Thus, jail administrators and local government officials will need to explore alternatives to increased spending in order to deal with the problems of physical plant replacement, personnel augmentation and program services implementation (Price and Newman, 1979).

Recently programs have been undertaken with the intent of reducing jail expenditures, while at the same time improving certain services for inmates. One method in which some jails have improved services while responding to budget cutbacks has been to reduce the population of the jail. This reduction has been aimed at pretrial inmates. By implementing a pretrial release program and personal recognizance programs, many jail systems have reduced the costs of inmate confinement because a proportion of food and housing costs for persons in these programs are picked up elsewhere. Total jail operational costs are thereby reduced.

The National Advisory Commission on Criminal Justice Standards and Goals (1973), in its report on local adult institutions, notes that both referral and more formalized diversion provide ways of reducing jail costs while providing greater opportunities for offenders by utilizing resources of other criminal justice agencies. Another method of cutting jail costs while increasing services for inmates was recognized by the National Sheriff's Association (1974). In its publication for jail administrators, authors note that few jails can provide all the services needed by incarcerated offenders. They recommend that jail administrators establish cooperative relationships with both public and private agencies that are able to provide needed services for jail inmates.

Given the realities of spiraling inflation on the one hand and cutback management on the other, more and more county jail administrators will attempt to manage more creatively in order to maintain programs that are necessary for inmates. Within this context, this project will analyze and report on two jail programs that have managed scarce resources to the benefit of inmates through imaginative management techniques.

Project Objectives

The intent of this project is to provide information to jail administrators who need to plan for and accommodate budget cutbacks while preserving critical services and programs. Information on problems, issues and solutions was obtained from jail administrators and personnel in two jurisdictions that experienced declining revenues while maintaining inmate programs or experienced inflationary costs that were higher than funding appropriations.

REFERENCES

Levine, C. (1978), "Organizational Decline and Cutback Management," pp. 462-481 in F. Lane (ed.), Managing State and Local Government. New York: St. Martins Press.

Levine, C. (1979), "More on Cutback Management: Hard Questions for Hard Times," Public Administration Review (March/April), 179-183.

May, P. and A. Meltzer (1981), "Limited Actions, Distressing Consequences: A Selected View of the California Experience," Public Administration Review, 41 (January/February), 172-178.

Miron, J. (1979), Training Strategy Paper on Managing the Pressures of Inflation in Criminal Justice, National Criminal Justice Executive Training Program, Washington, D.C. (March).

Murphy, P. (1971), "Police Accountability," pp. 35-49 in J. Wolfie and J. Heaphy (eds.), Productivity in Policing. Washington, D.C.: Police Foundation.

National Advisory Commission on Criminal Justice Standards and Goals (1973), Local Adult Institutions, Washington, D.C.: 273-288.

National Sheriff's Association (1974), Jail Administration. Washington, D.C.: 52.

Nelson, E. and N. Harlow (1980), Responses to Diminishing Resources: The California Experience, Report to N.I.C. (December), Washington, D.C.

Price, B. and C. Newman (1979), Multijurisdictional and State Jails: A Study in Organization and Management, National Institute of Corrections, U.S. Department of Justice (February), Washington, D.C.

Richmond, M. (1972), "Measuring the Cost of Correctional Services," Crime and Delinquency 18, (July): 243-252.

CHAPTER I

Local Government Finances

Before one can define strategies to deal with resource scarcity in jails, it is essential to describe those county financial arrangements that directly effect jail operations. Too often in past studies of jails, the relationship between county appropriations and jail operations have been ignored.[1] Therefore, it is important to provide some insights into local government finance, especially in these times of dwindling local revenues.

Until very recently, little attention has been paid to the subject of declining local government revenues. This is a new phenomenon for all levels of government, which in the past had concentrated on methods of public budgeting based on incrementalism and increasing revenues. Not many in the field of public finance were concentrating their efforts on actions that should be taken during substantial budgetary decline (Glassberg, 1978).

Tax Payer Revolts

Beginning in 1978 with California's Proposition 13, citizens across America voiced their sentiments about tax rates relative to service quality and voted for reduced taxes. Government budget cuts resulted, as did reviews and evaluations of existing public programs and the closer scrutiny of proposed new programs. As a consequence of the "taxpayer's revolt", governmental resources have become scarce. Many public programs have been reduced in scope or abolished in order to balance budgets. The era of unlimited financial resources based on increasing taxes has come to an end (Kemp, 1980).

A survey by the National Conference of State Legislatures (New York Times, 1979) showed that twenty-two states have cutback property taxes; fifteen states have curtailed sales taxes; eighteen have reduced income taxes; and eight states have voted for tighter spending limits. (See Table I)

---

[1]An exception to this is Billy Wayson, et al, Local Jails, which discusses the costs of implementing jail standards in the State of Washington.

Effects of Tax Cuts
on Local Governments

It is necessary to understand the manner by which local governments are financed before we can understand how county jails are effected by declining revenues. Property taxes are the most frequently used source of local government revenues with revenues from state sales tax, state income tax funds and federal aid constituting up to 40 percent. Because of this pattern of producing revenue, taxpayer revolts that effect income or sales taxes deplete the monies of local government more so than cuts in property taxes (Poole, 1980).

General sales taxes are more significant sources of local government revenue than are income taxes. Twice as many states use a general sales tax as opposed to an income tax (Due and Mikesell, 1975). Thus, when federal dollars are cutback at the same time that state and local tax revenues are decreasing, local governments find themselves in a genuine dilemma in meeting the demands for public service programs on the part of citizens.

Restrictions on local governments further hinder their capacity to generate resources. Local governments are subordinate to the state and must conform to its laws. This limits the autonomy of local officials. Ultimately, state laws govern state and local financial relationships (Florestano, 1981).

Local Government
Financial Dependence

With the ever increasing demands for increased and improved public programs, and with the dwindling sources of local revenue, financial aid will be requested from the states. This will be because of decreases in federal aid that local communities have become dependent on for many programs, as well as the consequence of limits on property taxes as a revenue producing priority for public services (Shannon, 1979).

TABLE 1

STATES CUTTING TAXES IN 1979

Property Tax Cuts - 22

Arkansas, Florida, Idaho, Iowa,
Kansas, Kentucky, Maryland,
Massachusetts, Minnesota,
Missouri, Montana, Nevada,
New Mexico, North Dakota,
Ohio, Oregon, South Dakota,
Tennessee, Utah, Washington,
Wisconsin, Wyoming.

Sales Tax Reductions - 15

Kansas, Kentucky, Maine,
Maryland, Michigan, Minnesota,
Mississippi, Nevada, New York,
South Dakota, Tennessee,
Tennessee, Virginia, West
Virginia, Wisconsin.

Income Tax Reductions - 18

Arizona, Colorado, Delaware,
Indiana, Iowa, Kansas,
Minnesota, Mississippi,
Montana, New Mexico, New York,
North Carolina, Oklahoma,
Oregon, Rhode Island, Vermont,
Virginia, Wisconsin.

Spending Limits - 8

Florida, Massachusetts,
Montana, Nebraska, Oregon
Nebraska, Oregon, Rhode Island,
South Carolina, Utah.

Property Assessment Curbs - 4

Arizona, Iowa, Maryland, Oregon

Note: Most states in which there was no action passed tax
reduction laws or amendments or spending limits during
1978. New Jersey, for example, has been struggling for
several years to live under ceilings on government spending
for state and local governments, first enacted by the
Legistlature in 1976.

Source: New York Times, August 5, 1979.

3

In past years local governments had increased their reliance on the federal sector for all types of aid. Table II illustrates this increased financial dependency by counties, cities, and school districts. Small and medium-sized cities had, by 1976, developed the lowest degree of dependence on outside fiscal aid compared to counties and large cities which had the greatest dependence. Overall, local governments as a whole showed a high dependency for outside monies (Lovell, 1981).

There has been a parallel trend of transferring governmental functions from municipalities to counties in recent years. Such transfers of services from one governmental unit to another occurs primarily when a smaller unit realizes that it is not financially able to provide a particular public service. The Advisory Commission on Intergovernmental Relations (1976) reported that for that year nationally, of 1,708 functional intergovernmental transfers, 56 percent went from municipalities to counties, 19 percent from states to special districts, and 14 percent from the federal government to the states. If this trend continues in the 1980's, county revenue bases will be further strained. A cyclical pattern emerges as the counties turn increasingly to state government for financial assistance while the states are forced to cut their own programs because of decreases in federal funds.

One nationally known program in criminal justice in which the state increased its funds to county correctional programs is the California Probation Subsidy. Instituted in 1965, the subsidy program gives money to those California counties that provide local correctional programs to offenders in lieu of having such offenders incarcerated in state facilities. The subsidy is actually based on performance measures. That is, it will increase its funds to a county if the reduction in state prisoner placements increases annually. A standard performance is expected in the program:

Not only must there be a commitment level from a county jail in order for it to be eligible for funds, but the county must also provide supervision services to probationers at an approved level in order to receive reimbursement (Wayson, et al., 1977: 77).

4

TABLE 2

FEDERAL AND STATE AID TO
DIFFERENT TYPES OF LOCAL GOVERNMENTS

Type of Jurisdiction	Fiscal Year	Federal and State Aid as Percentage of General Revenues from Own Sources
All localities	1977	75.4
Municipalities	1977	62.9
School districts	1977	97.4
All cities	1976	67.2
Less than 100,000 persons	1976	49.9
500,000 persons and over	1976	84.9
All counties	1976	82.3
Less than 100,000 persons	1976	88.1
100,000 to 2999,999 persons	1976	87.9
300,000 persons and over	1976	77.2

Source: ACIR, Significant Features of Fiscal Federalism, 1978–79 ed.,
          Washington, D.C., May 1979; U.S. Bureau of the Census, City
          Government Finances in 1975–76, Series GF76, No. 4, and County
          Government Finances in 1975–76, Series GF76, No. 8.

5

It will be interesting to see if Proposition 13 will eliminate the subsidy program in the future, even with the knowledge that incarceration in a state penal facility are higher per inmante than those of a probationer in the subsidy program. This may be a situation where the counties transfer a program back to the state, due to the counties' desire for less program responsiblity, even though state funds are provided in the form of a subsidy.

Local Government and
Criminal Justice

The Rand Corporation's study of the impact of Proposition 13 on local criminal justice agencies (1980) raises some vital issues for local officials and the citizens they represent. An important question raised in this study is whether the choices of local elected officials are also the priorities of the majority of their constituents. If no consensus exists, program cuts may anger voters. The potential for conflict is especially high for legally mandated vs. preferred programs. An example is the mandated implementation of jail standards by the courts vs. the preferred building of a new jail facility.

Mandated activities, including those that local officials feel are not a priority, will be absorbing and increasing amount of local government revenues. Voters who are opposed to these trends will find it difficult to hold local officials accountable, because the local elected representatives claim that they cannot legally resist the mandates (Walker, et al., 1980: 47).

In sum, local officials are torn between fulfilling legal mandates through greater public expenditures and meeting the community's desire for projects believed to be more important.

As mentioned previously, incremental additions to public budgets had been the financial philosophy underlying governmental budgeting practices. However, as a result of the inflation and recession of the 1970's, questions began to be asked about the effectiveness of public programs and about the accountability of public officials. Specific questions were raised concerning the effectiveness, efficiency and productivity of criminal justice programs in this period of economic decline (Miron,1979).

During this same period, national increases in the crime rate occurred. One result was higher expense for corrections, both at the county and state levels. Expenditures for corrections programs have not historically been particularly popular. With federal and state funding reduced, correctional programs and facilities will not, in most circumstances, be a high priority to public officials. Correctional administrators, thus, will need to develop innovative programs and utilize modern managerial techniques that will cut down costs and improve program performance.

Jails and Managerial Strategies

Census of Jails and Survey of Jail Inmates - 1978

More than 158,000 persons were held in the nation's locally operated jails as of February 1978 -- an increase of 12 percent over the 1972 total. The latest profile of jail inmates reflected the traditional, two-fold function of a jail: a place for the temporary detention of the unconvicted and a confinement facility where many convicted persons -- predominantly misdemeanants -- serve out their sentences. About six of every ten jail inmates had been convicted of a crime. In all, roughly three-fourths of such inmates had entered guilty pleas -- many after plea bargaining -- rather than standing trial. The remainder had been judged guilty. Compared with state and federal prisons, jails held a much smaller percentage of inmates for violent crimes, but larger proportions for property and public order offenses.

Some four out of every ten jail inmates stood accused but not convicted of a crime, and about one-fifth of this group did not have a lawyer at the time of the survey. Most of those who had counsel (82 percent) were being represented by court-appointed lawyers, public defenders, or legal aid attorneys. Four-fifths of all unconvicted inmates remained in jail even though bail had been set for them by the authorities.

7

Whites outnumbered blacks in the nation's jails, but the proportion of blacks in jail far exceeds their 12 percent share of the U.S. population. Inmates belonging to other minority groups accounted for some 2 percent of all jail inmates. As in 1972, the 1978 jail population consisted predominantly of males.

The vast majority of inmates were young men in their twenties. Three out of five had not completed high school, and 43 percent were jobless prior to being jailed. Not surprisingly, their reported average income was extremely low -- a median of only $3.255 during the year prior to arrest. One in four had a record of military service, most of them during the Vietnam era.

Sixteen percent of the inmates admitted to being regular heroin users, and another 10 percent had used heroin occasionally at some time during their lives.

Nearly half of the nation's 3,493 jails, holding about 43 percent of the inmates, were in the South. For every 100,000 inhabitants in the nation as a whole, there were 76 inmates held in locally operated jails. On a regional basis, the highest ratio was in the West, the lowest in the north central states. Among the 45 states having jails, Georgia, Nevada, Alabama, and Louisiana ranked highest in the ratio of inmates to population, but none of these states was among the top four in terms of the total jail population. California, Texas, New York, and Florida each held at least 10,000 persons in jail; California, with more than 26,000 inmates, held more than twice as many as each of the other states. (Source: National Prisoner Statistics Bulletin, National Criminal Justice Information and Statistics Service, Law Enforcement Assistance Administration, February 1979.) (See Table)

The national average population in our jails was 36 inmates per facility in 1972, but 74 percent of the 3,493 jails holding inmates longer than 48 hours accommodated twenty or fewer prisoners. Only 3 percent of the total number of jails housed 250 or more prisoners (The Nation's Jails, 1975). Excluding incarceration stays of less than 48 hours, an estimated three to five million persons spend time in the nation's jails each year, and that is ten to fifteen times the number of inmates handled by all state and federal correctional institutions annually (Goldfarb and Singer, 1973).

8

This country's jails were operated by 44,298 employees, 89 percent of whom worked full-time. Of the total work force, 46 percent were custodial personnel (guards and jailers), 27 percent were administrative staff, and 7 percent were professional program staff (The Nation's Jails, 1975).

Historical precedence, more than political, economic, or management logic, has placed the jurisidictional responsibility for jail operations at the local level of government with the ultimate budgetary decisions for its functioning in the hands of elected county officials (Wayson, et al., 1977). As illustrated by the following chart, in 1979 the nation's counties spent 27.3 percent of county government funds for criminal justice corrections programs. One can only speculate that since 1979, costs of jails and other correctional programs have risen, at minimum, at the rate of inflation. County government representatives realize that spiraling inflation, decreases in county revenues, and the growing crime rate, all combined, increase demands on county budgets. These same officials are looking to their criminal justice administrators to provide solutions to this complex dilemma. They are demanding that criminal justice agencies do more with less.

The Court and Legal Mandates
Effecting the Jail

After a long period of neglect, jails particularly have come under scrutiny. Courts have found violations of individual prisoners' rights. In the last decade the courts have been willing to intervene in jail administration and have made judgments that define the rights of persons incarcerated in our nations' jails.

A legal mandate is a requirement for local government to perform some activity on behalf of national or state policy objectives. In the case of jails, mandates usually take the form of court orders. The Rand Corporation's study on the impact of Proposition 13 on California's justice system found an important consequence of mandates in periods of fiscal contraction:

> Most mandates are underfinanced and the cumulate weight of numerous mandates is a great burden on local government . . . . When the revenue from local government is

9

TABLE 3

NUMBER OF JAILS AND JAIL INMATES - 1978

(By Region and State, and by Inmate Sex, Legal Status — Adult or Juvenile — and Ratio to General Population)

Region and State	Jails	All Inmates			Adults			Juveniles			Rate per 100,000 Pop.
		Total	Male	Female	Total	Male	Female	Total	Male	Female	
United States Total	3,493	158,394	148,839	9,555	156,783	147,506	9,277	1,611	1,333	278	76
Northeast	207	24,228	23,039	1,189	24,129	22,984	1,145	99	55	44	54
Maine	13	325	316	9	319	310	9	6	6	0	30
New Hampshire	11	370	347	23	362	340	22	8	7	1	43
Vermont*	-	-	-	-	-	-	-	-	-	-	-
Massachusetts	15	2,317	2,281	36	2,317	2,281	36	0	0	0	40
Rhode Island*	-	-	-	-	-	-	-	-	-	-	-
Connecticut*	-	-	-	-	-	-	-	-	-	-	-
New York	72	10,936	10,302	634	10,852	10,261	591	84	41	43	61
New Jersey	28	3,873	3,648	225	3,873	3,648	225	0	0	0	53
Pennsylvania	68	6,407	6,145	262	6,406	6,144	262	1	1	0	54
North Central	1,042	28,452	26,687	1,765	27,937	26,256	1,681	515	431	84	49
Ohio	150	5,465	5,109	356	5,377	5,035	342	88	74	14	51
Indiana	90	2,453	2,334	119	2,301	2,200	101	152	134	18	46
Illinois	100	5,781	5,499	282	5,758	5,476	282	23	23	0	52
Michigan	93	5,729	5,282	447	5,708	5,262	446	21	20	1	63
Wisconsin	70	1,926	1,806	120	1,864	1,767	97	62	39	23	41
Minnesota	65	1,517	1,431	86	1,504	1,421	83	13	10	3	38
Iowa	91	664	611	53	654	603	51	10	8	2	23
Missouri	137	2,849	2,668	181	2,829	2,652	177	20	16	4	60
North Dakota	39	118	105	13	117	105	12	1	0	1	18
South Dakota	44	276	258	18	253	243	10	23	15	8	40
Nebraska	77	676	647	29	638	611	27	38	36	2	44
Kansas	86	998	937	61	934	881	53	64	56	8	43
South	1,678	67,444	63,992	3,452	66,775	63,420	3,355	669	572	97	98
Delaware*	-	-	-	-	-	-	-	-	-	-	-
Maryland	25	3,553	3,418	135	3,553	3,418	135	0	0	0	86
District of Columbia	2	1,407	1,292	115	1,407	1,292	115	0	0	0	208

10

Region and State	Jails	All Inmates Total	All Inmates Male	All Inmates Female	Adults Total	Adults Male	Adults Female	Juveniles Total	Juveniles Male	Juveniles Female	Rate per 100,000 Pop.
Virginia	92	4,232	4,059	173	4,077	3,907	170	155	152	3	84
West Virginia	54	1,066	1,017	49	1,044	996	48	22	21	1	57
North Carolina	95	2,798	2,635	163	2,766	2,615	151	32	20	12	51
South Carolina	68	2,362	2,281	81	2,328	2,256	72	34	25	9	84
Georgia	223	8,278	7,933	345	8,269	7,925	344	9	8	1	165
Florida	112	10,305	9,615	690	10,263	9,576	687	42	39	3	122
Kentucky	111	2,149	2,024	125	2,089	1,968	121	60	56	4	62
Tennessee	111	4,553	4,330	223	4,492	4,287	205	61	43	18	106
Alabama	108	5,049	4,903	146	5,027	4,883	144	22	20	2	137
Mississippi	94	2,427	2,310	117	2,359	2,260	99	68	50	18	102
Arkansas	92	1,334	1,261	73	1,277	1,211	66	57	50	7	62
Louisana	93	5,232	4,996	236	5,217	4,985	232	15	11	4	134
Oklahoma	102	1,704	1,550	154	1,676	1,529	147	28	21	7	61
Texas	296	10,995	10,368	627	10,931	10,312	619	64	56	8	36
West	566	38,270	35,121	3,149	37,942	34,846	3,096	328	275	53	100
Montana	58	324	304	20	304	289	15	20	15	5	43
Idaho	45	539	508	31	498	477	21	41	31	10	62
Wyoming	31	268	243	25	244	230	14	24	13	11	66
Colorado	61	1,681	1,598	83	1,658	1,576	82	23	22	1	65
New Mexico	38	794	741	53	755	711	44	39	30	9	67
Arizona	39	2,501	2,163	338	2,484	2,150	334	17	13	4	108
Utah	24	676	643	33	675	642	33	1	1	0	53
Nevada	22	912	821	91	896	810	86	16	11	5	144
Washington	59	2,453	2,273	180	2,437	2,257	180	16	16	0	68
Oregon	48	1,872	1,750	122	1,855	1,737	118	17	13	4	78
California	135	26,206	24,036	2,170	26,093	23,927	2,166	113	109	4	120
Alaska*	6	44	41	3	43	40	3	1	1	0	11
Hawaii	—	—	—	—	—	—	—	—	—	—	—

* Five States — Connecticut, Delaware, Hawaii, Rhode Island and Vermont — had integrated jail-prison systems and, therefore, were excluded in calculating the rate of inmates per 100,000 population at the regional and national levels. Alaska, which had six locally operated jails in addition to an integrated jail-prison system, was included in the calculation.

Source: National Prisoner Statistics Bulletin, National Criminal Justice Information and Statistics Service, Law Enforcement Assistance Administration, No. SD-NPS-J-6, February, 1979.

11

prevented from increasing to meet the increased costs of mandates, local officials face a serious problem of compliance (Walker, et al., 1980).

Court orders have attempted to remedy jail conditions, such as sanitation, population, administrative procedures, and physical plant maintenance. Jail administrators have been under great pressure to conform to court orders while operating under severe economic constraints (Smykla, 1981). As a result of court cases, standards have been developed that attempt to set miminum conditions under which prisoners can be incarcerated in a safe and healthy environment.

Jails will require a better articulated rationale for the implementation of standards, and the ends to be achieved by them, difficult and sometimes unpopular choices of priorities, and judicious allocation of scarce resources (Wayson, et al., 1977: 17).

The bind of meeting health and safety standards with reduced resources is one that cannot easily be resolved. The building of a new physical plant or renovation of an older jail facility is costly. Implementation of human service programs is also costly. Even more problematic, as described earlier, is the reluctance on the part of the public to spend scarce dollars on projects that havve a low priority among citizens of the community. Yet, there are legal mandates imposed by the courts or, at minimum, jail standards that have put pressure on jail managers which need to be complied with to some extent. According to Smykla (1981), the problems of jail administrators are as follows:

1. Developing services;
2. Delivering services;
3. Finding qualified personnel; and
4. Adequate funding.

This author goes on to point out that jails in rural areas encounter some problems that are more unique to rural than urban facilities. Rural jails, notes Smykla, must deal with a population that is widely scattered. This fact often causes rural jails to have difficulty recruiting adequate staff, providing

FIGURE 1

COUNTY GOVERNMENT CRIMINAL JUSTICE EXPENDITURES

$4.7 Billion

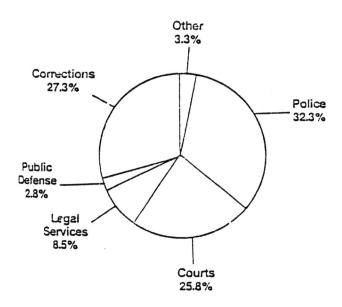

Source: Sourcebook of Criminal Justice Statistics:
February, 1979, NILECJ.

programs and obtaining equipment -- all of which are more readily available in urban areas. This often results in increased costs for facilities and personnel. Usually rural jails are small and do not have industry which produces tax revenues. Because rural jails are located in sparsely populated environments, the county does not have access to large revenues produced by sales, property, or business taxes. "The burden of financing local jails is disproportionate; therefore, sufficient funds are not appropriated." (Wayson, et al., 1977: 14)

A recent study of jail programs for narcotic addicts (Newman and Price, 1977) found that the major concerns of jail administrators included:

1. Current organizational and operational aspects of the jail;

2. Nature of the jail population in terms of transcience;

3. Tendancy of courts to intervene in jail administrative activities;

4. Administrative focus of jails -- that is, law enforcement or corrections;

5. The funding base and the availability of external funding sources;

6. The quality and quantity of community based human service resources;

7. The nature of the interface between the jail and other units in the criminal justice system;

8. The community's attitude concerning punishment and treatment;

9. Tradition of community volunteering; and

10. The locus of jail control.

Of all these concerns "... the issue of where the needed financial resources were to come from was found to be the most important." (Newman and Price, 1977: 179) It is a long established fact that jails have been among the lowest priorities for county funding since the days when John Howard inherited the jail at Befordshire in 1773. (Allen and Simonsen, 1981)

Is there any resolution to the foregoing problems of depleted county revenues, citizen apathy about jail conditions, implementation of standards for our nations' jails and numerous court orders that require improvements in all aspects of jail operations? There are resolutions, but many traditional modes of jail operation will have to change. Jail managers will clearly have to provide the leadership and coordination for the design of innovative programs. In the past, administrators of jails were confused by the effects of court cases and the implementation of jail standards. Their typical approach was reactive. Long-term attempts at improving efficiency and effectiveness were secondary to the crisis management behavior that prevailed. (Corrigan, 1979)

Now, with the pessimistic finanancial future, it is of utmost importance that jail administrators expand their managerial skills and capabilities by making modifications in administrative and managerial techniques. Above all, jail administrators must become pro-active and learn to plan ahead for their jails. Managers in this day and age must become coordinators of services and lobbyists for their facilities and programs. In sum, they must gain citizen support for those programs which they believe to be essential to the progressive operation of the jails which they manage and they must be skillful administrators with respect to internal jail operations.

Obstacles to Innovative
Management Techniques

Research by Levine (1979), Berman and McLaughlin (1977), suggests that political, organizational and systemic obstacles are likely to prevent innovative management in times of reduced operational budgets. An important conclusion of the research is that whether fiscal cutbacks lead to innovation and improved efficiency or whether local government services deteriorate depends primarily on the way in which government bureaucrats react to the changed economic circumstances.

Probably the most prevalent factor which precludes innovatave management strategies is the belief on the part of public administrators that this period of fiscal distress is only temporary. This reaction to our current economic situation is what Levine terms the "tooth fairy syndrome".

> In the initial stages of contractions (cutbacks) few people are willing to believe that the talk of cuts is for real or that cuts will be permanent. The initial prevailing attitude in the organization will usually be optimistic; i.e., that the decline is temporary and the cuts will be restored soon by someone -- in some cases as remote as the tooth fairy . . . . The preferred tactical response for nearly everyone is to delay taking action while waiting for someone else to volunteer cuts or for a bailout from a third party. (Levine, 1979: 181)

In the past, periods of economic uncertainty ended, or at least, appeared to improve over time. This optimistic manner of thinking does not seem to apply to our current fiscal situation. Inflation and its outcomes are permanent phenomena, and today's agency executives must not wait to take action in formulating managerial ingenuity in dealing with our modern theme of productivity, which as an operational philosophy has permeated the public sector.

There are other impediments to implementing innovative management solutions to declining revenues. The former director of the California Department of Corrections, J. Enomoto (1979), is of the opinion that correctional administrators in the past have not taken the necessary initiative in evaluating their correctional systems for the expressed purpose of improving operations in a more economical way. Without program evaluation data, it is difficult to identify areas or administrative processes that might be improved.

The necessity to plan for the future has often been stated as an essential prerequisite for any organization that has to meet the demands for service. Unfortunately, many agencies in the public sector, including corrections agencies, have rarely heeded this essential administrative practice. At the local level, the response to cutbacks has been disappointing due to the lack of more comprehensive approaches to decreasing programs and services provided by public sector organizations (Kemp, 1980). As a

16

result of agency neglect in planning for troubled fiscal times, local officials are forced to cut agency budgets without very much planned input from agency heads. Kemp notes, local officials have not often planned ahead to develop sound approaches for declining revenues.

In this same context, another vital factor preventing innovate solutions is the lack of a rationale for deciding how to allocate diminished resources among competing programs. Decisions to cut should be based on prioritized organizational needs (Wayson, et al., 1977), but in the corrections field, both state and local administrators have been neglectful in using such strategies as management by objectives or program budgeting. Leaders in the corrections field have been reluctant to set specific goals, monitor performance and measure outputs in ways that would influence public opinion in a pro-active manner. Instead, they have merely responded to public demands in a reportedly defensive way (Corrigan, 1979). What correctional managers need to do is evaluate existing programs, redirect program priorities and improve and utilize technology in order to reduce the need for existing personnel. "If cutback management is to be implemented, there must be a shift from reactive administration to rational comprehensive management." (Corrigan, 1979: 59)

Jail managers must begin to define and communicate the jail's role within the criminal justice system and to ensure that their organization's mission and operational methods are valued by those public officials who have the power to provide or withhold resources.

County commissioners presumably are responsive to the public interest. They want to concentrate on problems that concern their constitutes. Corrections officials, on the other hand, may focus on improvements in the quality of services to clients; while county executives are concerned with costs and with setting priorities for competing budget demands. Such differences in goals, and in the values associated with them, set the stage for potential conflict in the change process and importantly, determine the character of the resulting organizational structure (Nelson, et al., 1980: 43)

17

County commissioners must be educated about the jail's attempts to manage with cost savings and sound managerial techniques. Below are seven essential factors which McTighe (1979) believes must be considered before a public organization can begin to plan managerial strategies in dealing with scarce resources:

1. Political attitudes. Plans for managing with less must include the concerns of elected officials.

2. Organization's mission. The mission will dictate what strategies will be utilized with shrinking resources.

3. Cause of resource decline. The strategies must respond to the immediate cause of reduction as well as take into consideration longer term solutions to problems of which the current cause of budget reductions may only be symptomatic.

4. Personnel system. The manager must be aware of the constraints the personnel system places upon the ability to scale down the organization before beginning with the development of a strategy.

5. Centralization. The more decentralized the organization, the more concerned the manager must be to include subordinate managers in strategy formulation.

6. Clientele. What role they play in the cutbacks -- are they vocal or passive.

7. Past stability. The response to cutbacks by employees will be conditioned by their prior exposure to similar circumstances.

Leaders of local correctional programs must reverse their existing reactive posture of waiting to see what their budget will look like before enacting services which are necessary for prisoner welfare. Several explanations exist for the lack of pro-active comprehensive planning on the part of agency administrators and for the lack of attention paid to educating elected officials. The most prevalent excuse is that agency administrators cannot foresee what elected public officials will do. Explanations such as this ignore the reality that what elected representatives will actually do or not do is often related to the amount of documented alternatives presented by correctional managers (National Advisory Commission on Criminal Justice Standards and Goals, 1973). In these times of fiscal austerity and agency accountability, managers must document their budgetary needs through the process of planned programming. The role for jail managers has expanded to include more than administering of day to day operations. Among their multiple responsibilities is the ever present necessity of planning, which in the long run will allow for a pro-active stance with respect to resources and program development.

Perhaps the greatest failure of corrections in the area of public politics is the shortsightedness of correctional administrators regarding the need for community support. This failure is applicable to all levels of corrections. Local correctional operations have rarely asked for or received public recognition for what they and their staffs do. Like state correctional systems, what publicity usually exists is negative. When inmate disturbances, fires, civil rights suits or hunger strikes occur, corrections has surfaced to the public limelight. Rarely has there been positive news concerning reintegration programs for inmates coming from correctional systems. Thus, citizens are ill-informed about positive correctional programs.

Because of there low public profile, jails are service providers without citizen support. They are probably the one county-funded agency that most community members would rather ignore. Thus, citizens do not push elected officials to appropriate funds to improve their corrections programs. Jails have been viewed as a political liability to county officials. The monetary constraints, notes Bartollas (198]), that are characteristic for corrections at the state level are equally, if not more severe, in county jails. As a result jail personnel are underpaid; the food budget is seen as an area in which to cut overall costs; funds for recreational equipment or programs for leisure-time activities are rarely available. "Part of the problem is that the jail lacks a political constituency because there are no votes in jails. Commissioners understandably favor such politically attractive institutions as hospitals and schools," (Bartollas, 198]: 220).

Despite these factors, Nelson, et al., (1980), in their study of local community corrections, concluded that there currently remains support for programs which focus on the resocialization of offenders. They claim that persuading the public, as well as its elected officials, for the need of such programs must be conducted in clear and convincing terms.

Modifications within local corrections comes in the midst of governmental reform with an emphasis on reducing costs, but in the long run justification for organizational improvements aimed at programs for offender resocialization must be legitimized through commitment and support of its own mission. (Nelson, et al., 1980: 116)

The implication here is that local corrections authorities must get their agency in order on an internal organizational level before they can convince significant decision makers of the benevolence of their mission. Once objectives have been clarified, the attempt to legitimize them must emanate from community support. The backing for program implementation and budgetary appropriations for corrections must begin with citizen involvement. At budget time, citizen advocacy could be the most crucial factor in determining funding priorities for corrections. This, in turn, could make all the difference between success or failure in working with those incarcerated in our nation's correctional institutions (West, 1979).

One explanation for the lack of community support for jails is their public image of doing little more than warehousing inmates. In order to gain support from the public, jails have to be viewed as a provider of services with a recognizable and legitimate mission. There are some (Wayson, et al., 1977) who believe that jail staff have no time to accomplish little more than booking and custodial functions. They note that this circumstance is the result of high prisoner turnover, which causes the majority of staff time to be spent on intake processes and leaves little time for individual treatment.

Wayson, et al., (1977) argue that prisoner turnover would be easier to manage if prisoners were more alike. They are of the opinion that because of the differences within the inmate population, ordinance violators, misdemeanants, and felons prevent the jail

20

from implementing a clear and decisive mission. The inmate population mix contributes to the jails' uniqueness which results in conflicting philosophies (detention vs. rehabilitation) and causes difficulty in operational management. Whether or not this problem can be solved, or should be solved, is clearly a complex issue. Obviously, the lack of a stable inmate population over lengthy periods of time has had a detrimental effect on jails not having a clear organizational mission. But, a lack of clear objectives and mission also applies to state correctional systems who have inmates confined in facilities for long periods of time and have been severely critized, especially in recent years, for not focusing their operations around an overall mission. Granted Wayson, et al., have a point when they state that jails have a large part of their population coming and going on a daily basis, but explanations such as this one for not focusing the organization's objectives based on an overall mission is one of the major reasons for the reluctance on the part of citizens to support the jails. What is necessary in order to gain citizen advocacy is relevance. If the role of local corrections can be modified to one which is seen as providing some solutions to the increasing crime problem, through attempts at resocialization of offenders, then perhaps citizens will begin to understand the relevancy of the jail. Modifying the detention image to one that includes resocialization programs will greatly assist the image of jails. It will expand the role of jail employees to one that reflects people managing, not just a people processing and warehousing role. Jail personnel must be prepared to meet these changing needs through training and administrative leadership (Pappas, 1971).

Jails, too, lack community support because of their isolation from other agencies in local criminal justice systems. Unlike other components of the justice system, which interact with each other more frequently, the jail remains a holding facility, an institution viewed by many as a dumping ground for those offenders who have failed to improve through the services provided by other agency programs. What is needed is for jails to beome an integrated part of the correctional system at the local level with close ties to probation and parole institutions. To do so, jails must begin to provide medical, educational and employment aid, together with programs that deal with the overwhelming problems for offenders caused by

21

alcoholism, drug abuse, and social alienation. (National Advisory Commission on Criminal Justice Standards and Goals, 1973). Further, the task of integrating services for offenders housed in jails will have to include the use of other community resources outside of the criminal justice system. It is clear that, in the past, treatment methods for offenders required a long period of time. Knowing that a large number of jail prisoners are incarcerated for a short period of time, it is necessary to implement programs that utilize the resources of community agencies to make sure that those offenders who have participated in programs in the jail continue to receive help upon returning to the community (Newman and Price, 1977).

If the role of the jail is expanded to one which includes attempts at offender reintegration, then its visability within the county will increase. The advantages for such an expanded role are unlimited, especially for the benefits derived through integrated agency use of resources within the county which would prohibit the need for the jail to operate all of their own programs at increased costs.

REFERENCES

Advisory Commission on Intergovernmental Relations (1976), Pragmatic Federalism: Reassessment of Functional Responsibility. Washington, D.C.: U.S. Government Printing Office.

Allen, H. and C. Simonsen (1981), Corrections in America. New York: MacMillan.

Bartollas, C. (1981), Introduction to Corrections. New York: Harper and Row.

Berman, P. and M. McLaughlin (1977), The Management of Decline: Problems,Opportunities, and Research Questions. The Rand Corporation, Santa Monica, California.

Corrigan, M. (1979), "Cutback Management in Corrections," Going into the 80s: Coping with the Pressures of Diminishing Resources. The annual meeting of the Conference of State Criminal Justice Planning Administrators, National Criminal Justice Executive Training Program, Washington, D.C.

Due, J. and J. Mikesell (1975), "Local Sales Taxes and Income Taxes," J. Aronson and E. Schwartz (eds.), Management Policies in Local Government Finance. Washington, D.C., International City Management Association.

Enomoto, J. (1979), "California Copes with Taxpapers' Revolt: The Sky Hasn't Fallen on Corrections," in the proceedings of the 109th Annual Congress of Corrections, The American Correctional Association, Philadelphia; 232-238.

Florestano, P. (1981), "Revenue-Raising Limitations on Local Government," Public Administration Review, 41 (January): 122-130.

Goldfarb, R. and L. Singer (1973), After Conviction. New York: Simon and Shuster.

Glassberg, A. (1978), "Organizational Responses to Municipal Budget Decreases," Public Administration Review, (July/August).

Kemp, R. (1980), "Cutback Management: Coping with Revenue Reducing Mandates," <u>Management Information Service Report</u>, 12 (July), 1-9.

Lovell, C. (1981), "Evolving Local Government Dependency," <u>Public Administration Review</u>, 41 (January) 189-201.

May, P. and A. Meltzer (1981), "Limited Actions, Distressing Consequences: A Selected View of the California Experience," <u>Public Administration Review</u>, 41 (January)`, 172-178.

McTighe, J. (1979), "Management Strategies to Deal with Shrinking Resources," <u>Public Administration Review</u>, (January/February) 86-90.

Miron, J. (1979), <u>Training Strategy Paper on Managing the Pressures of Inflation in Criminal Justice.</u> National Criminal Justice Executive Training Program, Washington, D.C. (March).

National Advisory Commission on Criminal Justice Standards and Goals (1973), <u>Local Adult Institutions</u>, Washington, D.C.

National Criminal Justice Information and Statistics Services (1979), <u>Census of Jails and Survey of Jail Inmates</u>, U.S. Department of Justice, Washington, D.C.: U.S. Government Printing Office.

Nelson, E. and N. Harlow (1980), <u>Responses to Diminishing Resources: The California Experience</u>. Report to N.I.C. (December), Washington, D.C.

Nelson, E. et al., (1980) <u>Program Models: Unificiation of Community Corrections</u>, N.I.J., U.S. Department of Justice.

Newman, C. and B. Price (1977), <u>Jails and Drug Treatment</u>. Beverly Hills: Sage Publications.

Pappas, N. (1971), <u>The Jail: Its Operation and Management</u>. Federal Prison Industries, Lompoc, California.

Poole, R. (1980), <u>Cutting Back City Hall</u>. New York: Universe Books.

Shannon, J. (1979) "Our Changing Federal-State-Local Fiscal System," presentation before the National Institute of Public Affairs Seminar, Washington, D.C. (January).

Smykla, J. (1981), Community Based Corrections. New York: MacMillan.

The Nation's Jails (1975), A Report on the Census of Jails from the 1972 Survey of Inmates of Local Jails. Washington, D.C., U.S. Government Printing Office (May).

Walker, W. et al., (1980), The Impact of Proposition 13 on Local Criminal Justice Agencies: Emerging Patterns. Rand Corporation, Santa Monica, California (June).

Wayson, B. et al., (1977) Local Jails. Lexington: D.C. Heath.

West, P. (1979), "The Taxpayers' Revolt and California Corrections," proceedings of the 109th Congress of Corrections, American Correctional Association, Philadelphia, 239-243.

25

Strategies for Managing Scarce Resources

The following is not meant to prescribe particular management strategies for those who run jails and are facing declining fiscal resources. Rather, it is intended as a beginning step in the process of developing managerial techniques to cope with an uncertain budgetary future. There is no one strategy that will enable managers to meet the needs of all prisoners while operating under diminishing resources. All jails face certain common problems. But, there are circumstances unique to particular local corrections agencies that prevent the implementation of a single universal management strategy.

Mobilizing the Support of
County Elected Representatives

All jail managers should be cognizant of the fact that their particular institution is within the public domain and, therefore, is affected by local politics. Because of this circumstance, county jails are often accountable to not only the sheriff who is elected, but also to county officials who control jail operations through resource appropriations.

It is no secret that law enforcement functions in sheriffs' departments take precedence in budgetary matters over jails. Jails, as stated earlier, have a negative image as perceived by county commissioners. These officials have found through past experience that corrections at the local level are abundant with problems and offer few successes (Nelson, et al., 1980). It is understandable why these same county officials are reluctant to implement programs for law violators. Their constituents have usually been unwilling to fund programs to improve prisoners' opportunities to become productive citizens.

County commissioners experience the tensions of reconciling the demands of district constitutents with countywide interests and needs. With local functionings, staffing, and budgets increasing rapidly in recent years as a result of revenue sharing, incessant pressures to do more are accompanied by

strident demands to economize. Local
officials bear the brunt of public
indignation about perceived failures and
extravagances of government. The process
through which decisions are made regarding
new programs, reorganization, and funding
level is open, contentious, and volatile
(Nelson, et al., 1980: 116).

It is apparent that if jails are to fulfill their
ever increasing responsibilities, those who manage them
must be sensitive to the political priorities that are
important to elected county representatives. That is,
external pressures that directly effect the operation
of the program must be understood and planned efforts
on the part of jail managers to participate in the
selling of their facilities' needs to local
representatives is imperative.

As previously mentioned, the role of the jail
administrator has greatly expanded. Both internal
operations and external demands require managers to be
more than merely custodians which in the past was the
major function for jail administrators (Corrigan,
1979). Jail managers, according to Corrigan, have the
following responsibilities:

1. In security the job requires not only a
    knowledge of the jail, but it also requires
    an understanding of new technologies;

2. Jail managers must understand budgeting
    techniques;

3. They must be knowledgeable of the various
    types of treatment techniques and accept such
    programs as a vital service provided by their
    organization;

4. They must be knowledgeable of the law and the
    legal demands that affect jails; and

5. The awareness of marketing strategies and the
    use of public relations techniques, as well
    as political savvy, are necessary for
    managers to know in order to gain acceptance
    for needed resources and implementation of
    innovative managerial methods for the purpose
    of providing services.

Initiating Productivity Improvements

The Municipal Yearbook (1975) outlined the types of productivity improvements which were being employed by various city and county governments. Among the general listing of types of improvement strategies were: MBO, performance based budgeting, productivity measurement, work planning and control, employee incentives, productivity bargaining, private contracting for services, technological innovation, and performance auditing. Underlying the use of such techniques was the idea of increased and improved services for available resources. Implicit in these productivity improvement strategies was the assumption that local governments could improve or increase their service capacity within the limits of annual incremental increases in selected program budgets. Since 1975, however, the financial picture has changed. Incremental budgets have never kept up with increases in inflation and as a result public agencies are asked to perform even more efficiently than a few years ago. Productivity concerns have led to hard decisions for public administrators, but it has also forced managers to utilize innovative skills for organizational management.

One method of increasing or improving public services without increasing personnel and/or costs is that of implementing productivity strategies. The focus of productivity improvement techniques centers on the reallocation of decreased resources for the expressed purpose of increasing prioritized objectives (Miron, 1979).

In order to improve productivity a definition of the term is essential. The National Commission on Productivity (1973) suggests the following:

1. Improving productivity means improving current practices to the best level known, to get better performance without a proportionate increase in cost;

2. Improving productivity means allocating resources to activities which give the highest return for each additional dollar spent;

3. Given the uncertainties in criminal justice services definitions, productivity increases

means increasing the probability that a given objective will be met; and

4.   Improving productivity means making the most of the talents and skills available.

Obstacles to Productivity Improvement

One of the main impediments to organizational change and productivity improvement is staff resistance. Many tactics can be utilized to increase the likelihood that personnel will accept innovative program modifications geared toward operating with less resources. The National Commission on Productivity (1973) discusses such barriers to productivity. Their focus was on police departments, but we will utilize much of their insights as they relate to the operation of jails. In sum, utilization of their report is applicable to all public organizations and will be modified to apply to jail administration.

Any attempt to implement innovations that would increase productivity without obtaining commitment and input from employees can lead to counterproductive results. Furthermore, the fact exists that there are concrete personnel practices, which are deeply ingrained in the tradition of sheriffs' departments and cannot be rapidly changed. Attempts to modify personnel policies most likely will encounter resistance on the part of employees.

What the Commission advises is to avoid a "frontal attack" on the obstacles to innovative techniques:

Rather, a far less disruptive approach is to identify leverage points through which behavior can be effected. For example, if leaders could be exposed to more ideas, accompanied by more honest and evaluative information and precedents of successful implementation by other departments, they would probably become more flexible in their thinking. A department's leadership might thereby become more active in seeking better practices and more receptive to change. Another leverage point is the rate of successful innovation actually experienced. Better selection and management of innovative programs and more constructive relationships with outside helpers would increase the likelihood of success. That, in turn, would provide impetus for the success building on success phenomenon (p. 67).

In addition, the Commission suggests:

1. In general, there should be greater emphasis on incremental changes. Often, too much time, effort, and money are spent on sweeping changes that are too great a departure from traditional operating procedures. Radical program changes should be phased in through a series of evolutionary steps.

2. There currently exists few unbiased information sources regarding the evaluation of attempted innovative programs of jail cutback strategies. This greatly increases the risks inherent in trying something new, and increases the skepticism with which outside ideas are received. What is needed is an independent evaluation agency to help in the change process.

3. A survey of innovative jail programs should be undertaken that describes the innovations and various experiences that the jails surveyed had in implementing them. By doing this, the impetus for organizational change can be made more visible, and the increase of successful innovations can be expected and the lessons of shortcomings can be shared so others attempting program modifications will be made aware of the pitfalls of certain practices.

4. Those jails that tend to lead in the adoption of new ideas should be identified. Their key role in the innovation diffusion process should be formalized by publicizing their activities and establishing exchange programs so that they can help evaluate and offer suggestions for program change to other jails. A study should be conducted to determine what factors differentiate these progressive jails and allow them as leaders in jail administration to set precedence so other jails can follow suit.

5.   Training programs for jail staff should be
      established with a focus on the concept of
      planned change, management of change, and the
      evaluation of new ideas. The creation of a
      national corrections officer academy should
      be seriously explored. Such a program could
      have a great deal of prestige as a source of
      ideas.   It   could   contribute   to   the
      professionalism of officers at all levels of
      corrections   and   to   their   perception   of
      themselves as professionals. It could be an
      important source of badly needed managerial
      and technical skills.

The Commission goes on to make suggestions that
help _maintain_ programs and sustain their success once
they have been implemented. Again, it should be stated
that the Commission's efforts were directed at police
departments but generalizations can be made and applied
to the administration of jails.

The Commission notes the following:

1.   It is important to select programs that at
      least seem to be more productive in achieving
      a   jail's   objectives   than   just   any   jail
      activity. This point is especially true if
      the jail is using some of its own resources
      rather than requiring funding from outside
      resources.

2.   Jail administrators and staff need to have a
      realistic idea of the time delays before new
      programs   can   become   productive   and   to
      understand   the   necessity   of   protecting
      programs from allowing others to dissipate
      their resources before higher productivity is
      achieved.

3.   Citizens of the community must be educated
      about innovative programs so that they will
      be   more   tolerant   of   decreases   in   other
      responsibilities that the jail has provided
      due to the reallocation of resources.

4.   Jail personnel must be educated about the
      goals   of   innovative   programs   and   the
      improvements they are expected to produce in
      the   operations'   total   performance.   The
      educational process should permit employees

to give feedback concerning their opinions about new programs, as well as provide the oppportunity to make suggestions for improvement.

5. New programs should be carefully designed and evaluated so that, whether they are permanently adopted or dropped, those participating will have gained a learning experience from their successes or failures. Adequate evaluation can also help in revealing the effectiveness of controversial programs and help to maintain them in the face of opposition.

Utilizing Research and Development Personnel

Very little research has been conducted on the effectiveness of services provided by jail programs (Newman and Price, 1977). This lack of research means that the outcomes of particular innovations cannot be evaluated according to program goals.

Nelson, et al., (1980) in their study of community corrections, notes the problem of financing local correctional programs as a vital issue. They are of the opinion that any organizational program change is tied closely to adequate provision of financial resources:

> Because of the intergovernmental nature of funding decisions among public programs, corrections finds itself in a situation of diminished revenues and shifting resource allocations. Research needs to study the advantages of state vs. local funding, the pros and cons of block-grants, different formulas for administrative subsidies, and the delicate process of tieing financial aid to performance standards (Nelson, et al., 1980: 158).

In many administrative decisions, personnel in the area of research and development are considered a luxury in comparison to other employees in budgeted lines. When cutbacks are demanded, those working in research and development should become more crucial members of the organization rather than less. A major part of their task is to inform executives, through rigorous research, just where the agency has been most and least effective. Personnel reductions in this needed area, claims Walker et al., (1980) in discussing the effects of Proposition 13's impact on criminal justice agencies, means that data necessary for the identification of organizational problems including planning and management do not exist. Thus, needed data is not available for agency leaders as they make vital decisions that effect the organization. Further, notes Walker, et al., planning tools cannot be developed or implemented; creative personnel who could provide long-term solutions for critical agency problems are not being retained or kept abreast of new information; and most important, innovative techniques to meet organizational responses to decreases in funding are not being developed and implemented.

The impact that research personnel could have on the effective administration of jails is vast. For instance, as Nelson et al., have discussed, research in relating finances to performance measures can be a critical tool for convincing county executives of the need to maintain certain jail programs. In managing with scarce resources, those who appropriate funds have the right to request concrete evidence regarding operational effectiveness and efficiency. Both on an internal (operational) and on an external (community) basis, research and development personnel can be the provider of information. This information, in turn, can be used to steer the jail in a clear direction.

Establishing Objectives and Program Priorities

After studying one West coast state's jails, Wayson, et al., (1977) drew the conclusion that there exists a lack of policy objectives, and, where they do exist, they are vague without structure. This tends to ". . . make it difficult to answer the inevitable question of resource needs and to decide on specific resource allocations" (p. 102). As is obvious, managerial skills are probably as important to the efficiency and effectiveness of jails as the financial resources provided for their operations. The most critical difference between effective and ineffective criminal justice agencies today was to be found in their management capabilities" (Baird, 1980). As stated previously, administrators in local corrections have to utilize innovative managerial techniques before any improvements can be realized. This means that jail administrators might incorporate the principles and techniques of management by objective or cost-benefit analyses or, in some cases the tools of organization development.

Any drastic change in the administration of jails, despite their management capabilities, cannot be rationally determined unless the values underlying jail operations are understood by all and are clearly stated (Nelson and Harlow, 1980).

Levine (1979) has outlined two categories of tactics for organizational change in this era of cutback management. The first are tactics to resist decline; the second are methods to smooth decline. While some of the following tactics have little relevance for jails, they are offered here as representative of current trends for managing programs in times of declining resources.

Tactics to Resist Decline	Tactics to Smooth Decline
1. External (Problem Depletion) Political	
1. Diversify programs, clients and constituents	1. Make peace with competing agencies
2. Improve legislative liaison	2. Cut low prestige programs
3. Educate the public about the agency's mission	3. Cut programs to Politically weak clients
4. Mobilize dependent clients	4. Sell and lend expertise to other agencies
5. Become "captured" by a powerful interest group or legislator	5. Share problems with other agencies
6. Threaten to cut vital or popular programs	
7. Cut a visible and widespread service a little to demonstrate client dependence	
2. Economic/ (Environmental Entropy) Technical	
1. Find a wider and richer revenue base (e.g., meteropolitan reorganization)	1. Improve targeting on problems
2. Develop incentives to prevent disinvestment	2. Plan with preservative objectives
	3. Cut losses by distinguishing between capital investments and sunk costs

35

Tactics to Resist Decline	Tactics to Smooth Decline
3. Seek foundation support	4. Yield concessions to tax-payers and employers to retain them
4. Lure new public and private sector investment	
5. Adopt user charges for services where possible	

3. Internal   (Political Vulnerability)
   Political

1. Issue symbolic responses like forming study commissions and task forces	1. Change leadership at each stage in the decline
	2. Reorganize at each stage
2. "Circle the wagons," i.e., develop a siege mentality to retain esprit de corps	3. Cut programs run by weak subunits
	4. Shift programs to another agency
3. Strengthen expertise	5. Get temporary exemptions from personnel and budgetary regulations which limit discretion

4. Economic/   (Organizational Atrophy)
   Technical

1. Increase hierarchical control	1. Renegotiate long-term contracts to regain flexibility
2. Improve productivity	
3. Experiment with less costly service delivery systems	2. Install rational choice techniques like zero-base budgeting and evaluation research
4. Automate	3. Mortgage the future by deferring maintenance and downscaling personnel quality
5. Stockpile and ration resources	
	4. Ask employees to make voluntary sacrifices like taking early retirements and deferring raises
	5. Improve forecasting capacity to anticipate further cuts
	6. Reassign surplus facilities to other users
	7. Sell surplus property, lease back when needed
	8. Exploit the exploitable

The National Criminal Justice Executive Training Program on "Managing the Pressures of Inflation in Criminal Justice," categorized emerging cutback strategies as the following: (Fitzharris, 1979: 36-37)

Things you can stop doing:

1. Personnel cuts
2. Attrition
3. Freezes
4. Service or program cuts
5. Shedding traditional responsibilities

Things you can get others to do:

1. Transfer of services
2. Contracting*
3. State takeover of funding

Things you can do more efficiently:

1. Productivity improvements
2. Alternate approaches to service delivery
3. Service consolidation
4. Leasing
5. Centralization
6. Time controls

Ways to reduce labor costs:

1. Reclassification
2. Simplification of tasks
3. Increase use of civilians
4. Paraprofessionals
5. Volunteers

Ways to substitute capital for labor:

1. Computer
2. Facility improvement

*Currently, many are proposing that contracting out for public services can supply at least a partial answer to the financial problems of local governments (Bish and Ostrom, 1973). A few research projects conducted during the last few years indicate that some shifting of functions from the public to the private sector has occurred (Fisk, et al., 1974).

Whatever tactic(s) a jail manager selects, it is crucial to remember that any plan of action must take into account the local political environment. Public officials must be convinced of the potential benefits of innovative organizational strategies to manage decline. In sum, despite how unique and manageable new techniques may appear to those administering government funded programs, it is essential that these leaders not swim against the tide of public and political sentiment in the struggle to gain community approval.

REFERENCES

Baird, C. (1980), National Institute of Corrections, presentation to panel on research, American Correctional Association Annual Meeting. San Diego, (August).

Bish, R. and V. Ostrom (1973), Understanding Urban Government, American Enterprise Institute for Public Policy Research. Washington, D.C.

Corrigan, M. (1979), "Cutback Management in Corrections," Going into the 80's: Coping with the Pressures of Diminishing Resources, The Annual Meeting of the Conference of State Criminal Justice Planning Administrators, National Criminal Justice Executive Training Program, Washington, D.C.

Fisk, et al., (1974) Private Provision for Public Services. The Urban Institute, Washington, D.C.

Fitzharris, T. (1979), Probation in an Era of Diminishing Resources, National Institute of Corrections, Washington, D.C., (October).

Levine, C. (1979), "More on Cutback Management: Hard Questions for Hard Times," Public Administration Review, 39 (March/April): 179-183.

National Commission on Productivity (1973), "Barriers to Productivity Improvement in Law Enforcement," Washington, D.C.: 65-70.

Nelson, E.K. and N. Harlow (1980), Responses to Diminishing Resources in Probation: The California Experience, report to N.I.C. (December).

Newman, C. and B. Price (1977), Jails and Drug Treatment. Beverly Hills: Sage Publication.

Walker, W., et al., (1980), The Impact of Proposition 13 on Local Criminal Justice Agencies: Emerging Patterns. Rand Corporation, Santa Monica, California (June).

Wayson, B., et al., (1977), Local Jails, Lexington: D.C. Heath.

CHAPTER III

Methodology

The primary purpose of this research project, "Managing Scarce Resources for Jails," was to identify and access ways in which jails can function more effectively in an era of fiscal restraints. This study focuses on the following objectives:

1. Through the use of a structured interview schedule, to relate the events that led to innovative program management strategies in two county jails.

2. To describe successful attempts that have enabled jail services to be more efficient and effective.

3. To explore the relationships of jails to other units of local government (both political and administrative).

4. To describe future directions the two jails will be taking in order to maintain programs as fiscal resources further diminish.

The goal is to determine why some jails do better than others in managing scarce resources and how they accomplish what they set out to do. The questions we will attempt to answer include: How and under what circumstances have managers of jails been successful in maintaining programs when there have been threats to the operation? What innovative organizational changes have they made? What managerial techniques have they implemented? What type of fiscal strategies have they successfully utilized? What political or interagency agreements have they arranged?

A case study method was used. Data were collected from each jail's staff and from key persons in the community knowledgeable about the jail's programs. Other necessary data from budgets, documents, contracting agreements, etc., were used in order to verify the degree of diminished fiscal appropriations.

It must be stated that research of this nature (case study approach) has been critized for not providing hard emperical evidence to substantiate its findings. However, there are those who believe that this qualitative approach is not without merit:

> Qualitative and interpretive studies lack the reassuring certainty associated with the collection of hard data, but they too have an important role to play, dealing as they do in the same kinds of elusive and inconsistent facts that managers of complex organizations must work with, studies such as this may be especially useful to the practitioner in understanding and responding appropriately to the kaleidoscope world he faces everyday (Nelson and Harlow, 1980: 73).

A primary concern of this particular research endeavor is to relate the successes and failures of two jail programs in order that other local corrections jurisdictions may learn from their experiences. The case study approach seems a most appropriate method to obtain data relevant to those in positions who could profit from the experiences of others.

Selection of Two Jails

The two jails that were selected for our research projects were selected according to the following criteria:

1. They had to be providing services to inmates before and after their budgets were reduced, or the annual appropriations for the jail had to be lower than the rate of inflation;

2. The facility had to be representative of county jails nationally. That is, they had to be operating under a sheriff and funded through a county;

3. Jails had to be known to the staff of N.I.C. Jail Center for having innovative programs or innovative managerial strategies;

4. Sheriffs and jail managers needed to be cooperative and willing to allow their organizations to be studied. They further needed to arrange interviews with significant people both internal and external to the organization.

42

Research Instrument

A structured interview schedule was designed. Each person interviewed was asked questions on the following five subject headings:

I.   Forces that Affected Jail Administration

   A.   What Local Influences Did the Jail Face?
        1.   Tax Base for Jail Support
        2.   Cooperating Community Agencies
        3.   Political -- County Commissions and Budget
        4.   Citizen Attitudes

   B.   What State Influences Existed?
        1.   Standards
        2.   Funding
        3.   State Court Decisions
        4.   Contracting Services
        5.   Inspection
        6.   Political-Legislative Mandates

   C.   What Federal Influences Affected the Jail?
        1.   Federal Court Decisions
        2.   Technical Assistance
        3.   Federal Projects Funding

   D.   Were There Influences From the Professional Community?
        1.   Treatment Ideologies
        2.   Training Participation
        3.   Standards

   E.   What Impact Did Community Attitudes Toward the Jail Make?
        1.   Political Climate
        2.   Attitudes Toward Criminals
        3.   Education of Public About Needed Programs and Maintenance of Jail Standards
        4.   Participation and Support of Community Groups
        5.   Attitudes Toward Funding

43

F.   What Impact Did Jail Employee Groups Have on Cutback Management and Jail Operations?
1.   Level of Support for Programs
2.   Attitude of Employee Organizations

II.   Under What Conditions Were Jail Services Provided?

A.   To What Extent Did Standards Exist and Were Applied?
B.   How was Personnel Utilized?
C.   Was There a System of Personnel Classification and Personnel Records?
D.   To What Extent was There Community Participation in Jail Programs?
E.   What Inmate Services were Provided?
F.   What Inmate Activities Exist?
G.   What Programs Were Terminated?
H.   What Activities Were Assigned to other Service-Providing Agencies?

III.   What Planning Existed Regarding Budget Cutbacks?

A.   Was There Development and Expanded Use of Volunteers?
B.   Was There the Development of an Inmate Classification System that Enabled Better Management of Inmate Supervison?
C.   Was There Development of Public Education Efforts by a Pro-Active Use of Local Media?
D.   Was There Management Planning by the Sheriff and Jail Administrator in Anticipation of Budget Cutbacks?
E.   Did the Jail Administrator Establish Priorities and Study Jail Personnel in Order to Act Rather than React to Budget Cuts?
F.   Was the Establishment of Relations with Other Components of Criminal Justice System and County Commissioners Utilized in Order to Ensure Greater Understanding and Support for the Effects of Monetary cutbacks?

IV.   What Techniques Were Utilized by Jail Administrators?

A.   What Strategies Did Jail Managers Utilize to Overcome Budget Cutbacks?
B.   What Organizational Modifications Were Made?
C.   What Was Their Predominant Management Style?
D.   What Specific Fiscal Strategies Proved Effective?

E.   What Political or Administrative Alignments
     Did They Make?
F.   What Techniques Proved Successful for Selling
     Jail Programs to Local Government and the
     Community?

V.   What Were the Demographic Characteristics of the
     Jails?

A.   Political Jurisdiction
B.   Population of Area Served
C.   Geographic Area Served
D.   Unit of Government Responsible for Jail
E.   Daily Population of Jail - Pretrial and
     Sentenced
F.   Percentage of Inmate Population Time Served
G.   Nature of Physical Plant
H.   Adequacy of Jail Facility
I.   Personnel Employed

Each sheriff and jail manager was sent a copy of
the above questions prior to the interviews in order fo
them to have time to gather any documentation, budgets,
memorandum, etc. they believed would help in the
support of the study. It also was sent for the purpose
of familiarizing those interviewed with the type of
information that would be requested when the interviews
took place.

CHAPTER IV

Benton County Corrections System
Corvallis, Oregon

The Benton County Corrections Facility is located in Corvallis, Oregon which is the county seat. It is 85 miles south of Portland and 55 miles east of the Pacific Ocean. The city of Corvallis has a population of approximately 41,000 residents; the county approximately 69,000. In addition to Corvallis, there are three smaller communities in the county; Philomath with 2,800, Adair Village with 600, and Monroe with 500. The rest of the county's population reside outside these four communities. The county is known for its agricultural base, but light industry as well as Oregon State University (with a student enrollment of approximately 16,500 students) enhance the area. The university is located in Corvallis.

The Benton County Corrections Facility provides a case example of a jail's creative management in an era of diminishing resources. Built in 1976, its history is not without frustrations encountered nor mistakes made.

The leadership skills of Sheriff Jack Dolan and other community members have been exceedingly useful in developing and sustaining the kinds of citizen support that benefit those incarcerated in the County Corrections Facility.

Sheriff Jack Dolan was and is the force behind the entire corrections operation, which in Benton County has created genuine programs for offender resocialization. It has been this sheriff's philosophy to provide the offender with the opportunity to change. This has led to a corrections staff which values the development and maintenance of inmate programs, understands the needs for community support, values education, works well together as a team, and perceives the importance of compliance with national jail standards.

The following description of the Facility and its programs is largely the work of the Facility staff. Although edited somewhat by this writer, it accurately describes the Benton County Facility and has been substantiated by a site visit.

47

Mission Statement

In recognizing its responsibility to serve the community, the function of the Benton County Corrections Facility is to operate a safe, secure, and humane facility that adheres to all state standards for jail operation, American Corrections Association recommendations, and all considerations as provided by the United States Constitution.

The goal of the Benton County Corrections Facility is to provide and maintain a positive and professional atmosphere with emphasis on:

1. Providing for the basic psychological, physical, and medical needs of the inmate population.

2. Operating a variety of programs which provide inmates with the opportunity for successful reintegration into the community.

3. Insuring that all inmates are apprised of the Center's Rules and Regulations, and recognize their responsibility to act within them.

4. Providing inmates and staff with a safe, stimulating, and sanitary environment.

5. Recruitment and selection of professional staff.

6. Provide staff with continuing opportunities for professional education and training.

7. Facilitating community awareness and involvement in the Center's operation.

Physical Plant   (See Figure on page 49)

Prior to construction of the Benton County Corrections Facility, the philosophy was: "How small can we build the physical plant to effectively meet the community needs and maintain maximum security with a minimum number of staff?

The Benton County Corrections Facility was opened in November, 1976. The 10,000 square foot structure has a maximum capacity of twenty-seven residents with the capability to segregate females and provide limited segregation for juveniles. The Facility was designed

48

FIGURE 2

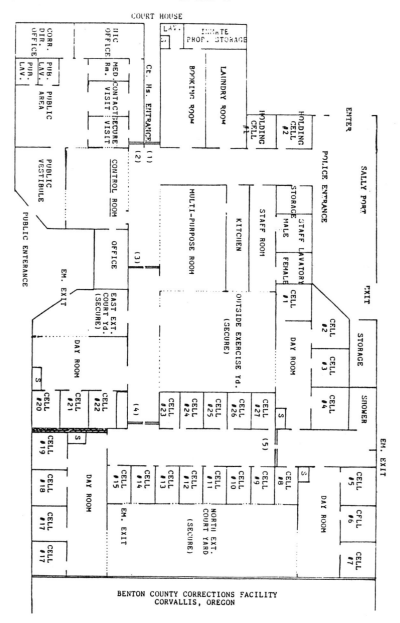

BENTON COUNTY CORRECTIONS FACILITY
CORVALLIS, OREGON

49

to enhance positive inmate attitudes through the usage of glass and open space. Openness, too, allowed for the reduction of custodial stations. Cells are single occupancy and feature natural lighting. The natural lighting is accomplished by sky lights or windows looking on to open courtyards with flowers and greenery. In the core of the Facility there is a screened outdoor courtyard available to the residents for exercise.

The Facility is centrally located in the Benton County-Corvallis business and government center. The law enforcement center, housing the Corvallis Police Department and the Benton County Sheriff's Department, is located directly across the street. The courthouse with district and circuit court facilities is located directly next to the Facility and is accessible through a secure corridor with visual and audio monitoring. Response time of law enforcement units to the Benton County Corrections Facility in emergency situations is less than two minutes.

The interior of the Facility has been painted in bright colors for aesthetic and therapeutic effects. All individual cell doors are color coded to correspond with the color code on the electronically-operated switchboard employed to open and close cell doors. Each cell is equipped with a stainless steel sink and urinal combination. Also, smoke detection devices have been installed in each cell that are not accessible to inmates. The smoke detectors are monitored by the city of Corvallis Fire Department, as well as in the Facility's control room. The response time of the Corvallis Fire Department to a fire or medical emergency in the Facility is approximately two minutes. Throughout the Facility, audio communications and video equipment are used, except in the four cell-block areas that have their own showers, where only audio is installed. The Facility is equipped with a variable fresh air control device through which air can be completely exchanged in fifteen minutes.

Intake

The Facility has recently installed a Regional Automated Information Network (RAIN) System for intake procedures. All intake information is entered into a terminal and displayed on a video screen in the booking room. The data are entered into computer files for storage and future retrieval. Designed to serve a all federal, state, and municipal clients, in accordance with the guidelines of the Community Corrections Act. The Facility works cohesively with the Community Corrections Advisory Board in identifying current needs for offenders, and giving direction to community corrections programs.

The Board is comprised of city and county law enforcement agencies: the Director of Local Corrections, a member of the local Bar Association, the Benton County District Attorney, the Circuit Court Judge, two interested citizens representative of the Oregon State Department of Corrections, and one ex-offender.

The population of the Benton County Corrections Facility is governed by a number of variables including statutory mandates, judicial prerogatives, inmate population constraints, and community action. However, in statistical terms, the Corrections Facility is represented by the accompanying data:

Table 4
Inmate Population Data: 1980-1981

Average Daily Population	25.6 - Capacity 27
Average Length of Stay	4.3 days
Female Population was approximately	10.1% of Total

The Benton County Corrections Facility operated during fiscal 1980-81 on a budget of $506,086. This included physical plant operation, inmate supervision, community corrections, misdemeanant parole and probation, and volunteer staffing.

Personnel Management

The Benton County Corrections Facility has a participatory management philosophy; all staff members have input into policy and procedures adopted. Supervision is provided by the Director and the Assistant Director of Corrections.

The line staff is comprised of four functional positions: Security Officers, Corrections Officers, Misdemeanant Parole and Probation Officers, and a Volunteer Coordinator.

1. Security Officers: Must fulfill high school educational requirements; be capable of

51

all federal, state, and municipal clients, in accordance with the guidelines of the Community Corrections Act. The Facility works cohesively with the Community Corrections Advisory Board in identifying current needs for offenders, and giving direction to community corrections programs.

The Board is comprised of city and county law enforcement agencies: the Director of Local Corrections, a member of the local Bar Association, the Benton County District Attorney, the Circuit Court Judge, two interested citizens representative of the Oregon State Department of Corrections, and one ex-offender.

The population of the Benton County Corrections Facility is governed by a number of variables including statutory mandates, judicial prerogatives, inmate population constraints, and community action. However, in statistical terms, the Corrections Facility is represented by the accompanying data:

Inmate Population Data: 1980-1981

Average Daily Population	25.6 - Capacity 27
Average Length of Stay	4.3 days
Female Population was approximately	10.1% of Total

The Benton County Corrections Facility operated during fiscal 1980-81 on a budget of $506,086. This included physical plant operation, inmate supervision, community corrections, misdemeanant parole and probation, and volunteer staffing.

Personnel Management

The Benton County Corrections Facility has a participatory management philosophy; all staff members have input into policy and procedures adopted. Supervision is provided by the Director and the Assistant Director of Corrections.

The line staff is comprised of four functional positions: Security Officers, Corrections Officers, Misdemeanant Parole and Probation Officers, and a Volunteer Coordinator.

1. Security Officers: Must fulfill high school

educational requirements; be capable of interacting with inmates on a daily basis; and are not required to supervise shifts.

2. Corrections Officers: Must hold a four-year degree; be capable of inmate supervision; and are responsible as shift supervisor.

3. Misdemeanant Parole and Probation Officers: Must hold a four-year degree; be capable of supervision of parolees and probationers assigned by the County: and function with limited direct supervision.

4. Volunteer Coordinator: Must hold a four-year degree; be capable of the recruitment, placement, and training of all forms of a volunteer corrections personnel; limited supervision of volunteers may be required.

Volunteer Program

The volunteer and intern worker is a valuable resource. "Volunteers" are of many types:

1. Volunteer: Interested local citizens who provide assistance in education, food preparation, arts and crafts, and religious activities.

2. Interns: Local college and university students who represent a wide array of academic interests and function in the Facility as working members of the corrections team.

3. Reserve Corrections Officers: Local citizens who exhibit a high degree of interest and dedication to the corrections center concept and regularly participate in the daily Facility operations.

4. Practicum Students: College and university students who operate much like the "student teacher" might in a classroom environment, with placements being approximately nine weeks of full-time participation.

Not only did these people contribute over 5,400 hours last year to the Facility, they are sources of contact for the residents to the outside community. Upon acceptance, all groups indicated above receive extensive training with the Corrections Facility. The training consists of all phases of the criminal justice system, including intake and discharge procedures.

After the volunteer/intern is proficient in the policies and procedures of the Facility, Benton County is unique in its treatment of these people. They are given the same opportunities to work with the inmate population that exist for the line staff.

Inmate Programs and Services

A variety of services and programs are available to inmates; including education, work release, recreation, medical and mental health care, library, and religious services. Community resources provide many of the services; a local community college provides G.E.D. classes, in addition to college accredited courses; the State Department of Vocational Rehabilitation and a local union provide educational and vocational opportunities; and the local YMCA makes it swimming pool and billiards room available. Work release is available to qualified sentenced inmates.

Medical. Medical services are provided for inmates by the Benton County Health Department and Good Samaritan Hospital. A county medical doctor makes calls to the Facility once a week and is on call at all times to provide medical treatment and consultation. In addition, a registered nurse is available in the Benton County Corrections Facility ten hours per week. Records kept by the nurse are recorded and filed by volunteers who work sixteen hours per month.

Mental Health. The Benton County Mental Health Program offers direct treatment and evaluation services to the inmates of the Benton County Corrections Facility.

Direct treatment can involve counseling on a regular basis (weekly) with inmates who request counseling themselves or who are recommended for counseling by the court. Brief interviews with DUII (Driving While Under the Influence of Intoxicants) inmates regarding alcoholism and treatment options and assisting inmates with treatment transitions to community programs upon release are also accomplished through the mental health staff.

54

Evaluation services include formal evaluations requested by court and informal feedback to mental health psychologists from the corrections personnel.

The Mental Health Department also devotes consultation and training time to the corrections staff. Case discussions and recommendations to staff on an informal basis, information and education on drugs and alcohol abuse, psychotherapy and treatment, and input in the interview/hiring process of new Corrections Facility personnel are provided by Benton County Health Department personnel.

Benton County Mental Health personnel devote approximately six to eight hours of their time to the Corrections Facility per week.

Education. The Adult Education Program is provided by Linn-Benton Community College. Regular college accredited classes are available, as well as G.E.D. classes. Other resources providing educational opportunities are the Department of Vocational Rehabilitation and the Adair union-sponsored vocational programs. Among the Adair programs, an applicant can enter carpentry, surveying, and masonry vocations.

Work Release. Benton County Corrections sponsors the release program and assesses it to be a successful method for the qualified resident to reenter the community with minimum supervision. The participants in the program have a sense of accomplishment and pride, as well as financial reward. Past participants have established bank accounts and made payments toward restitution and personal debts. The program is supervised by one corrections officer designated the School-Work Release Coordinator. With help from the reserve and intern staff, this program is of high priority within Benton County Corrections Facility.

Staff-Resident Assignment Programs. The philosophy of this program is that those effecting the greatest positive growth are those that have consistent interaction with the residents.

In order to provide meaningful growth opportunities, it is imperative that long-term residents of a correctional center be provided the opportunity and the environment for constructive personal growth and self-fulfillment.

The method used in this counseling program is based on:
1. Needs assessment profile of each resident.
2. Program plan and implementation for each resident.

The process of assigning a new resident to a staff member is based on the number of residents already assigned, the needs assessment profile for that resident, and then determining which staff member could best provide services to that resident.

Other Programs. These include the use of the local YMCA Chapter swimming pool by sentenced inmates. Library services are provided through the Corvallis-Benton County Public Library. In addition, recreative-rehabilitation programs are sponsored by local businessmen and various service and church organizations.

Personnel and Budget

The organizational chart of Benton County Sheriff's Department is illustrated on Page 61.

The Correctional Facility has seen a steady incline in institutional admissions, as well as an increase for the entire operation. The following data illustrates the increases in arrests within the entire county which directly effects the number of prisoners housed in the Facility from 1972 to 1980. Further, the budget for the operation of the Corrections Facility (not including external programs) has increased almost six-fold since 1972 through 1980.

The number of bookings in the county has steadily grown from 1972, experiencing a change of 136.8 percent in eight years.

Statistical projections estimate that by 1987-1988, the number of prisoners booked in Benton County Corrections Center could reach 4,287, an increase of 352 percent in fifteen years.

In a survey conducted of the previous fiscal year (July 1, 1979 through June 30, 1980), the total number of persons lodged was 2,247. Of these, 96.8 percent were adults. Traffic offenses were committed by 1,072 adults (49.3 percent); misdemeanors by 619 adults (28.4 percent), and felonies were committed by 484 adults (21.9 percent).

FIGURE 3

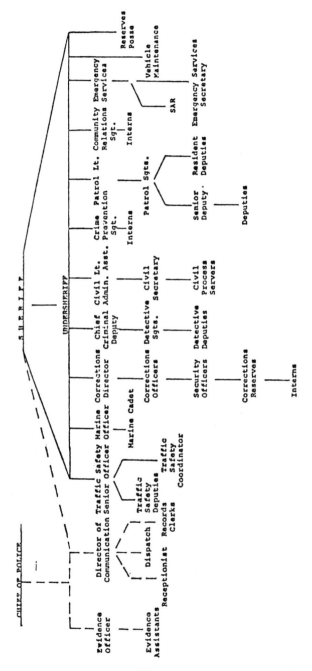

Table 5
Facility Budget

Year	72/73	73/74	74/75	75/76	76/77	77/78	78/79	79/80
Personnel	$31,838	$34,748	$28,908	$78,052	$108,929	$124,494	$192,126	$190,964
Materials/Service	$11,289	$17,005	$19,834	$24,263	$35,409	$33,838	$52,835	$69,810
Total	$43,137	$51,753	$58,742	$102,315	$144,338	$158,332	$244,961	$260,774

The average length of stay during this period was 3.8 days, reflecting an average daily population for the year of 27.7 (compared with capacity of 27):

If similar projection techniques are used as with the total jail population, it has been determined that an ADP of 57.6 might be expected by 1987-1988. This must be carefully interpreted -- many factors could intervene to assist in keeping this population down.

The single most frequent infraction committed by adults housed at the Facility is DUII, contributing to 55 percent of the traffic violations and 26.3 percent of all infractions. The traffic crime, DWS, is second, contributing 21.6 percent of the traffic violations and 10.4 percent of all incarcerations.

Table 7

Traffic Offenses

	Adults	Juveniles	Total	%
DUII	591	1	592	54.9%
DWS	232	1	233	21.6%
Warrants	141		141	13.1%
Operator License Violation	42		42	3.9%
Other Violations	29	1	30	2.8%
Leaving Scene of Accident	11		11	1.0%
Attempting to Elude	9	2	11	1.0%
Speeding	5		5	0.5%
Reckless Driving	5		5	0.5%
Careless Driving	4		4	0.3%
Defective Equipment	2		2	0.2%
Traffic Signal	1	—	1	0.1%
	1,072	5	1,077	

The major misdemeanor offenses are warrants, theft II, and disorderly conduct.

60

Table 8

Misdemeanor Offenses

	Adults	Juveniles	Total	%
Other Offenses	169	3	172	
Warrants 60	8	68		35.3%
Disorderly Conduct	46	2	48	9.9%
Theft II 42	1	43		8.8%
Assault IV	40	1	41	8.4%
Criminal Trespass	26	0	26	5.3%
Shoplifting	23	1	24	4.9%
Criminal Mischief	17	4	21	4.3%
Theft of Service	17	0	17	3.5%
Resisting Arrest	10	1	11	2.3%
Sex Offenses	8	0	8	0.8%
CAID	4	0	4	0.8%
NSF	2	0	2	0.4%
Possession of Stolen Property	1	1	2	
	465	22	487	

Felony convictions accounted for 18.5 percent of the incarcerations in 1979-80. The major reason for arrest and incarceration is warrants or burglary.

Table 9
Felony Offenses

	Adults	Juveniles	Total	%
Other Offenses	105	13	118	28.4%
Warrants	88	1	89	21.4%
Burgulary	53	20	73	17.6%
Theft I	42	3	45	10.8%
CAID	41	0	41	9.9%
Sex Offenses	19	0	19	4.6%
Robbery	8	3	11	2.7%
Murder	7	0	7	1.7%
Assault II	6	0	6	1.4%
Assault I	3	0	3	0.7%
Assault III	3	0	3	0.7%
	375	40	415	

Two hundred sixty-eight detox holds were made in the 1979-80 fiscal year.

Juveniles

Juveniles lodged at BCCF primarily have committed felonies (54 percent). The major felony crime committed is burglary (37.5 percent). One-third of the offenses committed by juveniles were lodged for traffic infractions.

Table 10
Bookings

The number of bookings in the county has steadily grown from 1972, experiencing a change of 137 percent in eight years.

Year

72/73	73/74	74/75	75/76	76/77	77/78	78/79	79/80

No. of Prisoners

949	856	1,117	1,355	1,982	2,269	2,129	2,247

% Change

N/A	-9.7%	+30%	+21.3%	+46.2%	+14.4%	-6.2%	+5.5%

County Revenues

Benton County has three elected county commissioners who are salaried and work full time. Taxes in the county are below those of many counties in the state of Oregon. The tax rate, though fluctuating from year to year, remains fairly constant. In 1971 the tax rate per $1,000 was a low $4.62. In 1976-77 the rate dropped to $4.48 on $1,000 of property assessment. The 1979-80 levy has a $3.51 rate. As one can see, the assessed property value levy has decreased somewhat in recent years at the same time the rate of inflation has increased, causing less revenue for county programs while increasing the expenditures of operation.

The county is provided with additional revenues from the Oregon and California Forest Revenue donation, a fund originally taken by the Oregon-California Railroad. This fund generated $2.5 million above and beyond the monies provided to operate county government generated by local revenue sources.

Benton County Lodging
Offense Type, 1972 to 1980

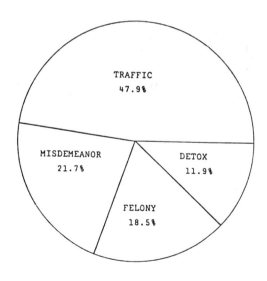

The property tax itself is based on assessed value that is regulated by state statutes and must be within 5 percent by state statutes and within 5 percent of true market value. The tax levy, based on a proposed budget, is drawn up by a committee of the three county commissioners and three citizens. Once approved by voters, this levy determines the amount the county needs to operate.

In 1979, Benton County began to receive funds from the State under the Community Corrections Act passed by the Oregon legislature. The philosophy of the Community Corrections Act is to subsidize county programs which take responsibility for those offenders at the local level of corrections instead of sentencing these offenders to state correctional institutions. The reimbursement is for Class C felons who have committed less serious criminal acts and can come under the supervision of local county corrections.

The Community Corrections Act requires all participating counties to have a community corrections advisory board whose membership is comprised of criminal justice personnel and private citizens. All budgetary requests for various programs (misdemeanant probation and parole, volunteer programs, and security and training is funded and approved by the advisory board). The advisory group also approves plans for future programs for local county corrections.

The Community Corrections Act (see financial summary table) has contributed $82,738 in 1979-80 and $171,940 in 1980-81 to the county for corrections. This financial summary further indicates a 43 percent projected increase in expenditures for the operation of corrections programs by 1983-84.

As one can clearly understand, Benton County will need to either appropriate increased county funds, even with the financial subsidy provided by the Community Corrections Act, or will have to cut down the number of staff, services and programs. Sheriff Dolan, in requesting future fiscal increases for corrections, will utilize planning projections based on data such as those described above.

TABLE 11
LAW ENFORCEMENT

FINANCIAL SUMMARY

	78-79 ACTUAL	79-80 ACTUAL	80-81 BUDGET	81-82 REQUEST	81-82 APPROVED	82-83 PROJECTED	83-84 PROJECTED	81-82 RECOMMENDED % OF 80-81 BUDGET
Fees	$ 32,816	$ 49,681	$ 56,920	$ 57,600	$ 61,560	$ 61,000	$ 64,100	8
General Purpose & Taxes	959,268	1,153,176	1,359,424	1,724,205	1,605,578	2,049,468	2,325,506	18
Program Generated Revenue	197,395	294,859	255,512	250,000	250,000	226,702	246,267	(2)
TOTAL REVENUES	$1,189,479	$1,497,716	$1,671,856	$2,031,805	$1,917,138	$2,337,170	$2,635,873	15
Personal Services	$ 972,126	$1,135,901	$1,306,027	$1,534,310	$1,466,543	$1,760,076	$2,035,347	12
Material and Services	175,840	292,104	324,112	438,745	421,745	490,094	536,526	30
Capital Outlay	41,513	29,796	38,717	55,750	25,850	83,000	59,000	(33)
Other Expenditures	0	26,246	3,000	3,000	3,000	4,000	5,000	0
TOTAL EXPENDITURE	$1,189,479	$1,484,047	$1,671,856	$2,031,805	$1,917,138	$2,337,170	$2,635,873	15
• • • • • • • • • • • • • • • • • • PERFORMANCE AREA EXPENDITURES • • • • • • • • • • • • • • • • • •								
801 Sheriff's Admin.	$ 59,493	$ 81,545	$ 95,573	$ 106,693	$ 104,347	$ 132,300	$ 130,...	9
802 Law Enforcement	589,205	671,357	733,935	1,052,295	994,098	1,249,918	1,415,192	35
803 Courts Enforcement	58,632	59,057	85,230	97,281	97,281	110,693	156,120	14
804 Support Services	171,818	217,571	186,662	0	0	0	0	(100)
806 Emergency Svcs	38,453	41,581	42,964	52,842	50,445	58,369	65,543	17
807 Corrections	271,878	330,198	355,552	558,074	507,602	603,231	664,481	43
808 Com. Corrections Act	0	82,738	171,940	164,620	163,365	182,659	203,787	(5)
Total Performance Areas	$1,189,479	$1,484,047	$1,671,856	$2,031,805	1,917,138	$2,337,170	$2,635,873	15

BUDGET ANALYSIS

Revenues:

The approved Law Enforcement budget has a general purpose fund increase of 18%. Part of this increase is due to a long term problem of fee revenues to keep pace with inflation.

Expenditures:

Overall expenditures are expected to increase $245,282 or 15%. This is due in part to personnel expenditures which have increased by 12%. This includes the addition of five new staff members in Corrections. The minimal increase is due to transfer of all personnel in the Records/Dispatch/ Reception support services to the City of Corvallis. This accounts for a part of the $97,633 increase in Materials and Services.

WP 1156/26

Planning for Community Corrections

Corrections in Benton County began to change in 1970 when Sheriff Dolan was elected. The strategies he and others utilized to construct a new corrections facility, as well as to implement community corrections programs, has been a struggle, but one that has seemingly been effective. The Sheriff's role in planning for the future of his total operation has always been significant and seems to indicate a direct force that has had major impact. All the improvements and program developments have been supported in large part due to the careful planning and political astuteness of Dolan and his staff.

The following work plans and objectives provide a good example of the type of strategic, comprehensive planning the Sheriff's Department has undertaken. Note that many of the corrections' objectives are for future implementation, which is indicative of a pro-active and futuristic managerial approach to attaining goals.

FIGURE 5

BENTON COUNTY
WORK PLAN
1981 - 1984

DRAFT!

PROGRAM: CORRECTIONS

DEPARTMENT: CORRECTIONS

SPECIFIC OBJECTIVE: CUSTODY (B07A)   PAGE 1

STATEMENT OF ONE-YEAR OBJECTIVES	PRIORITY	ACTIVITIES REQUIRED TO ACHIEVE OBJECTIVE	TYPE OF ACTIVITY BASE / ENH / NEW	EFFICIENCY AND EFFECTIVENESS INDICATORS FOR EACH OBJECTIVE OR ACTIVITY
OBTAIN AND MAINTAIN STAFF TO DEGREE RECOMMENDED BY NIC STAFFING ANALYSIS.	1	DEVELOP SCHEDULE THAT PROVIDES ADEQUATE COVERAGE FOR VACATION AND COMP. TIME. EXPAND RESERVE PROGRAM. PROVIDE UP-DATED STAFFING ANALYSIS TO FUNDING SOURCE.	81-84 / 81-84	IMPROVE TURNOVER RATE FROM 50% TO 15%
COMPLETE PHYSICAL PLANT MODIFICATION AND REPAIRS.	2	INSTALLATION OF NEW LOCKS. PERMANENTLY ASSIGNED MAINTENANCE STAFF. IDENTIFY DEFICIENCIES ON WEEKLY BASIS.	81-84	TIME REQUIRED FOR REPAIRS FROM POINT OF DISCOVERY. HIRING OF 1/2-TIME STAFF TO PERFORM DUTIES.
OBTAIN AND MAINTAIN ACA AND NWA ACCREDITATION.	3	COMPLETE POLICY AND PROCEDURE MANUAL. ESTABLISH COMMUNICATION AND SELF-ANALYSIS. SUBMIT APPLICATION FOR APPROVAL.	81-84 / 81-82	MEETING ACA DEADLINE SCHEDULE. COMPLETION AND OBTAINMENT OF CERTIFICATION.
ESTABLISH ADEQUATE EMERGENCY PROCEDURES.	4	COMPLETED POLICY AND PROCEDURE COVERING ALL AREAS. ESTABLISH AND IMPLEMENT TESTING SCHEDULE. PROVIDE STAFF TRAINING AND MONITOR RESPONSE PERFORMANCE.	81-84	NUMBER OF DRILLS COMPLETED.

FIGURE 6

BENTON COUNTY
WORK PLAN
1981 - 1984

DRAFT

PROGRAM: CORRECTIONS

DEPARTMENT: CORRECTIONS

SPECIFIC OBJECTIVE: CUSTODY (B07A)   PAGE 2

STATEMENT OF ONE-YEAR OBJECTIVES	PRIORITY	ACTIVITIES REQUIRED TO ACHIEVE OBJECTIVE	TYPE OF ACTIVITY		EFFICIENCY AND EFFECTIVENESS INDICATORS FOR EACH OBJECTIVE OR ACTIVITY
			BASE	ENH	NEW	
UPGRADE FOOD SERVICES.	5	CONTRACT MEAL SERVICE WITH OSU. IMPLEMENT BREAKFAST MEAL SERVED IN MULTI-PURPOSE ROOM.	81-84		
UPGRADE EXISTING INMATE PROGRAMS AND IMPLEMENT NEW PROGRAM AS INCREASED STAFFING WOULD ALLOW SUPERVISION.	6	USE VOLUNTEER STAFF THAT HAVE APPLICABLE SKILLS TO UPGRADE AND INITIATE PROGRAM ACTIVITIES. CORRECTIONS STAFF TO SUPERVISE PROGRAM ACTIVITIES.	81-84		EVALUATE QUARTERLY AS TO NUMBER OF INMATES PARTICIPATING IN INDIVIDUAL PROGRAM AREAS. MONITOR NUMBER OF INMATE INCIDENT REPORTS AS WELL AS DISCIPLINARY HEARINGS. SOLICIT RESPONSES FROM INMATES AS TO ACCEPTABILITY OF PROGRAMS.

68

FIGURE 7

		PROGRAM: CORRECTIONS
BENTON COUNTY **WORK PLAN** **1981 - 1984**		**DEPARTMENT:** LAW ENFORCEMENT **SPECIFIC OBJECTIVE:** CORRECTIONS, NIC RESOURCE CENTER (QU07E)

STATEMENT OF ONE-YEAR OBJECTIVES	PRIORITY	ACTIVITIES REQUIRED TO ACHIEVE OBJECTIVE	TYPE OF ACTIVITY			EFFICIENCY AND EFFECTIVENESS INDICATORS FOR EACH OBJECTIVE OR ACTIVITY
			BASE	CONT	NEW	
NIC PROJECT COORDINATOR TO BE PROJECT MANAGER FOR ACA ACCREDITATION.	1	DEVELOP CORRECTIONAL POLICY AND PROCEDURE. CONDUCT SELF-AUDIT OF CORRECTIONS FACILITY. REQUEST AUDIT FROM ACA CONSULTANT. FORMALLY APPLY FOR ACA ACCREDITATION.			81-84	MONTHLY AUDIT OF PROGRESS WITH ACA ACCREDITATION AT SEPTEMBER 30, 1981.
PROVIDE HOSTED TECHNICAL ASSISTANCE TO 15 INDIVIDUALS OR TEAMS.	2	RESPOND TO REQUESTS FOR HOSTED T.A. AS REFERRED BY THE NATIONAL JAIL CENTER.	81-84			NUMBER OF AGENCIES PROVIDED T.A. WITH COMPLETED ACTION AGENDAS. SIX-MONTH FOLLOW-UP WITH AGENCIES TO AUDIT PROGRESS OF ACTION AGENDAS.
PROVIDE "ON SITE" TECHNICAL ASSISTANCE TO 8 CRIMINAL JUSTICE AGENCIES.	3	RESPOND TO REQUESTS FOR ON-SITE T.A. AS REFERRED BY THE NATIONAL JAIL CENTER.	81-84			NUMBER OF AGENCIES PROVIDED T.A. WITH COMPLETED ACTION AGENDAS. SIX-MONTH FOLLOW-UP WITH AGENCIES TO AUDIT PROGRESS OF ACTION AGENDAS.
PROVIDE 3-5 DAY TRAINING SEMINAR FOR 25 JAIL ADMINISTRATORS FROM THE 8 WESTERN STATES SERVICE AREA.	4		81-84			USE OF PROFESSIONAL CRIMINAL JUSTICE CONSULTANTS TO PROVIDE TRAINING TO JAIL ADMINISTRATORS WITH WRITTEN EVALUATIONS BY PARTICIPANTS AS TO EFFECTIVENESS OF TRAINING.

69

FIGURE 8

BENTON COUNTY WORK PLAN 1981 - 1984 DRAFT I

PROGRAM: Corrections

DEPARTMENT: Corrections - CCA

SPECIFIC OBJECTIVE: Security & Training (B08A)

STATEMENT OF ONE-YEAR OBJECTIVES	PRIORITY	ACTIVITIES REQUIRED TO ACHIEVE OBJECTIVE	TYPE OF ACTIVITY BASE	ENH	NEW	EFFICIENCY AND EFFECTIVENESS INDICATORS FOR EACH OBJECTIVE OR ACTIVITY
Maintain staff/inmate ration of 2:25.	1	Provide adequate relief for sick and training time.	81-84			Overall staff/inmate ratio measured as of June 30, 1982.
Reduce by 50% the frequency of assaults on staff by inmates.	2	Increase staff supervision and communication. Reduce number of Disciplinary Hearings.	81-84			Number of incidents of assaults on staff. Number of inmate disciplinary hearings.
Provide Quarterly Training Sessions specifically addressing Benton County Corrections' needs and objectives.	3	Access training needs of staff. Poll staff to determine priority areas. Prepare and deliver sessions.		81-84		Number of training sessions provided.

FIGURE 9

BENTON COUNTY
WORK PLAN
1981 - 1984

DRAFT

PROGRAM: CORRECTIONS

DEPARTMENT: CORRECTIONS, 'CCA

SPECIFIC OBJECTIVE: MISDEMEANANT PAROLE AND PROBATION (MO80)

STATEMENT OF ONE-YEAR OBJECTIVES	PRIORITY	ACTIVITIES REQUIRED TO ACHIEVE OBJECTIVE	TYPE OF ACTIVITY BASE	ENH	NEW	EFFICIENCY AND EFFECTIVENESS INDICATORS FOR EACH OBJECTIVE OR ACTIVITY
95% SUCCESSFUL TERMINATION.	1	RE-EVALUATE CLIENT-CLASSIFICATION SYSTEM. INCREASED USE OF EARLY TERMINATION.		81- 84		DETERMINE THE NUMBER OF SUCCESSFUL TERMINATIONS.
INCREASE OFFICE COORDINATION/MANAGEMENT.	2	INCREASE ADMINISTRATIVE INVOLVEMENT. EVALUATE CURRENT AND PROJECTED SPACE REQUIREMENTS. OBTAIN ADEQUATE OFFICE SPACE. IMPLEMENT RAIN SYSTEM.	81- 84		81- 84	DETERMINE NUMBER OF HOURS MANAGEMENT PERSONNEL PARTICIPATES IN OFFICE ACTIVITIES. DETERMINE FREQUENCY OF RAIN USAGE AND COST OF USAGE.
COMPLETE POLICY AND PROCEDURE.	3	TOTAL STAFF PARTICIPATION IN THE WRITING AND REVIEW OF POLICY AND PROCEDURE MANUAL. PROVIDE POLICY & PROCEDURE MANUAL TO DISTRICT JUDGE FOR REVIEW.	81- 84	81- 84		AMOUNT OF POLICY AND PROCEDURE MANUAL COMPLETED BY JUNE 30, 1982.
INCREASE SUPERVISION AND SERVICES AVAILABLE TO CLIENTS.	4	PROVIDE 60 COMMUNITY SERVICE PLACEMENTS. PURCHASE SECOND VEHICLE. IMPLEMENT PROBATION FEE PROGRAM.	81- 84		81- 84	NUMBER OF COMMUNITY SERVICE PLACEMENTS. DID YOU PURCHASE SECOND VEHICLE? PERCENTAGE OF CLIENTS PARTICIPATION IN FEE PAYMENT AND DOLLARS COLLECTED.

WP SPO-B08B/11

71

FIGURE 10

BENTON COUNTY
WORK PLAN
1981 - 1984

DRAFT

PROGRAM: CORRECTIONS

DEPARTMENT: CORRECTIONS - CCA

SPECIFIC OBJECTIVE: VOLUNTEER PROGRAM (BOBC)

STATEMENT OF ONE-YEAR OBJECTIVES	PRIORITY	ACTIVITIES REQUIRED TO ACHIEVE OBJECTIVE	TYPE OF ACTIVITY			EFFICIENCY AND EFFECTIVENESS INDICATORS FOR EACH OBJECTIVE OR ACTIVITY
			BASE	CONT	NEW	
INVOLVE 84 VOLUNTEERS ANNUALLY IN LOCAL CRIMINAL JUSTICE PROGRAMS.	1	RECRUIT, SCREEN, TRAIN VOLUNTEERS. DEVELOP WORK CONTRACTS. DEVELOP INFORMAL PLACEMENT CONTACT WITH FACULTY, STAFF OF LBCC, OCE AND OSU.	81-84	81-84		NUMBER OF VOLUNTEERS RECRUITED.
PROVIDE ADEQUATE TRAINING, SUPERVISION AND SUPPORT TO VOLUNTEER STAFF.	2	OFFER EIGHT IN-SERVICE TRAININGS.	81-84	81-84		NUMBER OF TRAININGS OFFERED.
		PUBLISH SIX NEWSLETTERS. PROVIDE WORK SPACE FOR VOLUNTEERS.	81-84	81-84		NUMBER OF NEWSLETTERS PUBLISHED. ESTABLISHING WORK AREA FOR VOLUNTEERS.
		PROVIDE FUNDS FOR VOLUNTEERS TO ATTEND TRAINING, TRANSPORTATION, AND OTHER VOLUNTEER ACTIVITIES.		81-84		DETERMINE NUMBER OF VOLUNTEERS FUNDED AND COST PER PERSON.
		PROVIDE 1/2-TIME SUPPORT STAFF.		81-84		HIRE SUPPORT STAFF.
		DEVELOP POLICY AND PROCEDURES FOR VOLUNTEER PROGRAM.		81-84		HAVE WRITTEN POLICY AND PROCEDURES.
PROVIDE PUBLIC INFORMATION ABOUT THE CRIMINAL JUSTICE SYSTEM AND INCREASE THE VOLUNTEER PROGRAM TO 500 INDIVIDUALS.	3	PROVIDE MONTHLY ORIENTATION. SPEAK TO CLASSES AND COMMUNITY GROUPS.	81-84	81-84		NUMBER OF INDIVIDUALS ATTENDING ORIENTATIONS.

Local, State, and Federal
Influences Affecting the Jail

Influences that have had an impact on the corrections program in Benton County have emanated from multiple sources. Before Sheriff Dolan was elected, the League of Women Voters had been active in attempting to improve conditions in the county jail. When Dolan took office in 1970, he incorporated the League's interest in the problem into his own plans to improve the jail.

In 1970, the jail was an antiquated physical structure with very few human services provided for the inmates. At this time, the League of Women Voters was pushing for reform of the old facility. Simultaneously, a Corvallis city council member was attempting to get the city council involved in improving jail conditions. By aligning himself with the League and sympathetic city council members, Sheriff Dolan began to build on this support in order to gain political backing for the construction of a new correctional facility. (Such local support for his corrections programs continue to this day and he has expanded to include requests for funding of human service programs for offenders.)

Local forces thus existed that lent political support to the Sheriff in his attempts to operate a total corrections program. The impetus for drastic modification of county corrections began at the very beginning of the Sheriff's first term in office. The Sheriff in this case provided the leadership and coordinated various community constituencies for the construction of the new facility. Simultaneously, the Sheriff utilized this same community support to gain resources for new programs which were to benefit inmates and other offenders under his jurisdiction. The Sheriff's utilization of various citizen groups within the county has been in the past, and continues to be, an on going process, not one that diminishes with each issue that has been resolved.

By working closely with the League of Women Voters, Sheriff Dolan saw the opportunities that community support could provide, not only in the area of political support for the financing of a new institution and city-county building, but also in building a program for volunteer workers. The impetus for change in local corrections came mainly from the

Sheriff. It is he who executed internal pressures on past and present county commissioners through developing community support.

As stated earlier, jails are rarely a popular public priority. Sheriff Dolan continually plays the role of advocate for corrections. Because he has solicited and maintained public support for his past programs, he has a much easier time in gaining the support of county residents for new improvements. Such political pressure does have an effect on the decisions county commissioners make.

The commissioner interviewed for this case study, although characterized by the corrections staff as ultra-conservative, did state that he is greatly influenced by the public's support for certain programs as exemplified by the overwhelming bond issue vote to provide part of the funds needed to construct the new correctional facility. There were two bond issues for construction of a jail before Sheriff Dolan took office. Both attempts to gain voter support failed.

The Sheriff in Benton County is very aware of the need for public support and has consistently attempted to include citizens in his corrections programs, mainly through his volunteer program, which is proven to be cost effective as well as an avenue of direct contact between inmates and with community members. For every one dollar spent on volunteers, claims the Sheriff, he receives three dollars back. Therefore, volunteers provide a three-to-one payoff for his corrections operation.

The single most important influence the State of Oregon had on local corrections was the Community Corrections Act of 1977. It should be noted that the Sheriff was active in the movement to get the Oregon Community Corrections Act passed by the state legislature. This Act, discussed previously, has provided funds for community programs by subsidizing counties throughout the state that sentence Class C felons to local county corrections. The impact of such funding has helped enormously at the local level. Even with the Corrections Act's guidelines, it has allowed the Sheriff of Benton County flexibility to create and implement programs which, among other things, permit him to control the correctional facilities' population. The misdemeanant probation program, in cooperation with the judges, can put offenders on probation instead of incarcerating them for a given length of time. The parole program, also in cooperation with judges, permits inmates to be paroled under supervision (Class C felons). Sheriff Dolan is the chief administrator for these programs and has hired coordinators to administer them. However, all community corrections programs come under the direction of Jim Bachmeier, the Director of the Facility.

The ability to control the population of the Correctional Facility appears to be crucial in limiting the costs of incarceration.

L.E.A.A. and Other Federal Funding

The only influences on the county from the federal government was funding from L.E.A.A. for the planning of the new facility, and initial funding provided for the first years of the probation and parole program before the Community Corrections Act provided dollars.

Currently, the Corrections Facility serves as a resource center for the National Institute of Corrections (N.I.C.). With a grant from N.I.C. for $6,500, the Facility is applying for accreditation from the American Correctional Association in an attempt to meet national jail standards. This most arduous task is under the coordination of Sgt. Bill Linville, who also serves as the N.C.I. resource coordinator. It should be pointed out that Oregon does have state jail standards with a state inspector to monitor compliance. By all indications, this County Corrections Facility goes far beyond minimum compliance with state jail standards which seem to be much less demanding than those of the American Correctional Association.

Planning for Budget Cutbacks

Due to the political acuity of the Sheriff, together with vital community support, the corrections programs in Benton County have really not suffered severe budget restraints as yet. This is not to imply that the Sheriff receives all of the funding which he requests. In fact, it has been, and continues to be, difficult to get funding from the county commissioners for increased personnel that the Facility greatly needs. The Sheriff received funds for three new staff for the coming year after being understaffed since the new facility was opened. Again, the use of volunteers and student interns has always helped to strengthen personnel and will continue to provide needed manpower assistance in the future.

When the new facility was in its initial planning stages, it was acknowledged that the county's projected population increase would demand a second facility. The plan that was put forth involved construction of a new facility to house sentenced inmates in 1985. With the current fiscal status of Benton County, it seems that appropriations for this proposed construction will be difficult to acquire. A county-wide bond issue may be required to realize the new construction. Perhaps this struggle will offer Sheriff Dolan his greatest challenge since taking office.

It would be redundant to identify all of Benton County's correctional programs and their funding sources. However, there are some significant strategies that need elaboration. Because Sheriff Dolan has consistently pushed for corrections programs, he is not attempting to meet only minimum requirements. It is likely that even with resource scarcity, he will continue to expand his operation. He will do so by increasing program options using community resources in order to keep the Facility's expenditures from increasing too rapidly.

The Corrections Facility does have a classification system but it is mainly used for screening purposes for those inmates who may be in need of medical or mental health treatment. In the area of public education, we know how effective he was in educating the public for the passage of the bond issue which resulted in a new facility. Although the local newspaper has been less than supportive of the Sheriff and his correctional programs, his unique ability to gain public support through the use of educational techniques are frequently utilizied.

One point Sheriff Dolan stressed on several occasions was the importance of educating county commissioners about the issue of liability. To this date, there has never been litigation against the Sheriff's Department that resulted in monetary loss to the county. The Sheriff wants to maintain a clean record in this area and as part of his planning strategy, often reminds the three commissioners that the results of not being in compliance with correctional standards could lead to legal actions against them as well as himself. He furthermore argues that such sanctions could include punitive monetary damages for which they all are personally liable.

The possibility of law suits is very real, especially in the past few years where litigation against corrections on both the local and state levels has proliferated. Sheriff Dolan underscores this reality in his attempts to gain funding for improvements in the corrections programs. Raising the issue of liability appears to have been an effective process to some extent. However, it is difficult to isolate the effects of this strategy on funding decisions for corrections.

When discussing the financial drain that law suits could have upon the county -- a draw which would directly affect correctional operations -- Sheriff Dolan had an enlightened view:

> Law suits are going to force improvements in corrections. I look upon the law suits as a God's blessing. If I was one of the people being sued, taking money out of my pocket, maybe I'd look on it a little differently.

Sheriff Dolan further commented on the legal liability of county commissioners:

> The community shouldn't suffer as a result of bad management or not following constitutional minimum. The commissioners were obstacles for a long while until the liability was passed to them. Now they are learning how to pass that liability to the community. The community shouldn't have to suffer it either.

The county corrections program appears to have good relations with other components of the criminal justice system. The County Community Corrections Advisory Board, which requires representation of other criminal justice agencies in the county under state statute, is the formal coordinating mechanism. The Advisory Board is the agency responsible for disseminating the funds for the local criminal justice programs as provided by the State Community Corrections Act.

By its representation on the Advisory Board, the Sheriff's Department has access to judges, the prosecutor, probation officials, and others who make decisions about funding priorities. The Board provides the opportunity for all criminal justice officials in the county to exchange views and plan cooperatively for future needs.

The views that Sheriff Dolan expressed concerning the need to utilize other government agencies to assist the corrections programs are unique. When asked about how he intends to finance the proposed second facility, he replied:

> I recognize how hard it is to get dollars and I tend to believe that there are more efficient methods of providing service. I reckon it is going to be hard and the key is to continually be so involved with the community that they realize that these particular services are necessary and important. I know it will be hard to sell the local community on capital construction funds. That is one of the reasons why I put mosts of the eggs in the basket of going to the state and getting state legislation for state funds for capital construction.

One of the most informative techniques that this observer found in researching progressive jail administration was the development of a close association with state government officials -- both elected and administrative. Requests for funds went beyond the county level of government, and local state representatives were called upon frequently to support the Sheriffs' financial and statutory requests.

Management Style

The managerial style of the Sheriff and the Facility staff's director was one of participatory management. Sheriff Dolan commented on this point:

> Participatory management is a process I believe in. It's tougher to do, I think, but I think the end product, for example policy and procedures in the cop shop (law enforcement side) here to the whole department wrote the policies and procedures. It makes the

implementation of them so much easier. So I'm a participatory manager. In times of crisis I tend to become extremely autocratic just like any cop, and I realize that.

On more than one occasion, it was pointed out that Sheriff Dolan held a meeting outside the Facility where all problems of the Department were openly discussed. The meeting was voluntary and there was approximately a 90 percent attendance. The meeting lasted from 8 A.M. to 5 P.M.

As a result of this meeting, the Sheriff modified the organization of the department in order to ensure that corrections would not become secondary to law enforcement in the event a new sheriff took office.

What I've done, I've purposely set up a separate corrections component in the event that there was ever a sheriff elected that did not want to give the proper support over there. Then the three commissioners could take that entire program under their wing.

Another of the administrative strategies which the Sheriff implemented was to require corrections personnel to have college degrees. "Corrections officers" have to have bacheolor's degrees and the position is paid more than "security officers" which do not require the degrees. The hope is for a career-oriented personnel, rather than employees viewing their employment in the Facility as only temporary. Requiring a college education for all staff also tends to professionalize the corrections role and encourages corrections personnel to feel uniquely important within the total organization. The Sheriff commented:

I place a high emphasis on education. In the area of corrections that was the original intent of the job requirements. We cannot validate that a college degree is a necessity, but we found it desirable. Most of the successful applicants are people with a college education.

Corrections workers know that when they are hired, there is a carrer path for them in corrections. Employment in the Facility is not a stepping stone to road patrol, but it is rather considered a professional career with its own opportunities for advancement.

79

Perhaps, this more than any other factor, has tended to produce harmony between law enforcement and corrections employees. It should be noted that salaries are equal between law enforcement and corrections personnel, and both equally benefit from the employee association's collective bargaining agreements.

The corrections program in Benton County is managed on a daily basis by Jim Bachmeier. Both the Sheriff and the Corrections Director communicate frequently, and there appears to be shared responsibility for facility operations with the assistant director, Randy Fraser. One cannot help but notice the staff's age, which is quite young. Staff exhibited a genuine enthusiasm for their mission and view offenders in their charge as salvageable human beings.

Sheriff's Views on Offenders

Before we conclude the Benton County case study, it is necessary to describe why a sheriff, such as Jack Dolan, has fought so long and hard to provide services for inmates that go well beyond minimum standards. The leadership he and others have provided over the years is crucial if we are to understand the reasons why managing scarce resources has been so effective in Benton County.

Regarding the placing of inmates in programs and generating community support, Sheriff Dolan commented:

> My whole concept and the concept of community corrections is building small (the Facility) and then recycling the people faster. Getting them involved as soon as possible. Building advocates, maintaining social contacts between family and friends and so on. Do all of these things as much as possible.

Regarding Sheriff Dolan's veiws on the treatment of inmates:

> Corrections starts on the street with the police officer, and unless you have a system of both police and corrections people working together, you are not going to achieve your corrections goals. I think what happens in that Corrections Facility, if you

adversely treat people in there, the police
or the street are going to pay the price for
it.

The value of attempting to change offender
behavior was expressed by Sheriff Dolan as follows:

I don't know that the programs, that all
the things we are doing with prisoners, have
a great effect on them. But I know I'm not
damaging people to where they are worse than
when they came out.

Perhaps the following statement best characterizes
the philosophy of Sheriff Dolan and his entire
corrections staff: "We are change agents, and I enjoy
that label."

Conclusions

This particular case study has hopefully illustrated key factors that have been proven successful in
one county corrections program in an era of diminishing
financial resources.

The following summary indicates those factors
which have enabled county corrections to maintain
services for inmates as well as to attempt to meet the
requirements of national jail standards:

1. Consistent use of community support for the
   concept of community corrections;

2. Use of the political process at the county
   level to gain county funding for correctional
   programs;

3. Close association with state legislators who
   are on committees which deal with correctional issues;

4. Philosophy of corrections as a process to
   change offender behavior;

5. Equalizing correctional employees with that
   of law enforcement;

6. A constant effort to plan for future needs of
   corrections and to develop strategies to gain

funds for meeting departmental objectives;

7. Utilizing research in criminal justice as the basis for program development;

8. A belief in maintaining a small population within the Facility while using various programs that prove to be cost effective in limiting or avoiding incarceration of the majority of offenders;

9. Making use of other county and state agencies for the provision of services for offenders;

10. Developing a volunteer program which proves to be a cost saving device, as well as a method to maintain community support for county corrections;

11. Maintaining correctional issues with a high profile in the county through the use of the media and educational methods;

12. Keeping the Corrections Facility open for public scrutiny and sharing problems of facility operation with citizens;

13. Attempting to use participatory management techniques in order to attain staff input for problem solving;

14. Selection of young, educated personnel who believe in providing opportunities for self-improvement to offenders;

15. Close cooperation with other officials in the county criminal justice system for community corrections support;

16. Providing strong, visible leadership for corrections to the community;

17. Getting appointed to committees and being active in state associations that deal with correctional issues;

18. Being aware of federal funding for a short term basis to begin programs that, if proven successful, will be taken over by the county; and

19. Utilizing an administrative style which encourages scientific managerial principles for the purpose of operating a facility that attempts to meet constitutional standards and is cost effective.

The next few years will be a difficult time for Benton County, as well as other counties in this nation. When the state of Oregon actually feels the financial impact of the block grant programs from the federal government, it will be interesting to see how well county corrections will fair under more stressful fiscal constraints. However, with all the strategies Sheriff Dolan has utilized in managing county corrections, it is very plausible that his organization will be less affected by such fiscal constraints than the majority of other jail operations in the nation.

CHAPTER V

Hampden County Corrections
Springfield, Massachusetts

The Hampden County Jail and House of Correction is a ninety-three year old facility located in Springfield, Massachusetts. Springfield is an industrial city located in the western portion of Massachusetts, eighty miles from the Commonwealth's capital city, Boston, and three miles from the state of Connecticut. The population of Springfield is approximately 150,000 with the balance of the cities and towns within Hampden County adding an additional 150,000 residents. (See Population Table on page 92.)

The facility, under the administration of Sheriff Michael J. Ashe, has a rated capacity to house 256 inmates, both male and female, sentenced and pre-trial. It should be noted that the official title of the facility ". . . Jail and House of Correction" reflects two separate classifications of residents: "Jail" connotes pre-trial status and "House of Correction" implies a sentenced individual. Under present Massachusetts General Laws, an individual may be sentenced to serve a term of not more than two and one half years in the House of Correction for any one offense, although the Courts do have the option in multiple offenses to run the second and subsequent offenses either concurrently or consecutively (referred to in Massachusetts as "on and after" sentencing). At the present time, many of our House of Correction residents are serving sentences for offenses exceeding two and one-half years because of multiple offenses and the Court's desire to incarcerate for longer periods of time.

Table 12
Population of Hampden County

Cities and Towns Hampden County	Official Preliminary Figures*	State Census 1975
Agawam	26,281	24,305
Blandford	1,053	954
Brimfield	2,312	2,170
Chester	1,127	1,114
CHICOPEE	55,048	58,431
East Longmeadow	12,898	13,132
Granville	1,204	1,183
Hampden	4,749	4,571
Holland	1,594	1,347
HOLYOKE	44,819	46,790
Longmeadow	16,309	16,676
Ludlow	18,182	18,183
Monson	7,324	7,376
Montgomery	638	600
Palmer	11,410	11,755
Russell	1,564	1,580
Southwick	7,387	7,028
SPRINGFIELD	152,212	168, 785
Tolland	236	215
Wales	1,159	1,033
West Springfield	26,960	28,249
WESTFIELD	36,356	32,863
Wilbraham	12,062	13,139
TOTALS	441,884	461,659

*Changes pending U.S. Census 1980; only figures available on date of printing.

FIGURE 11

HAMPDEN COUNTY

636.11 Square Miles

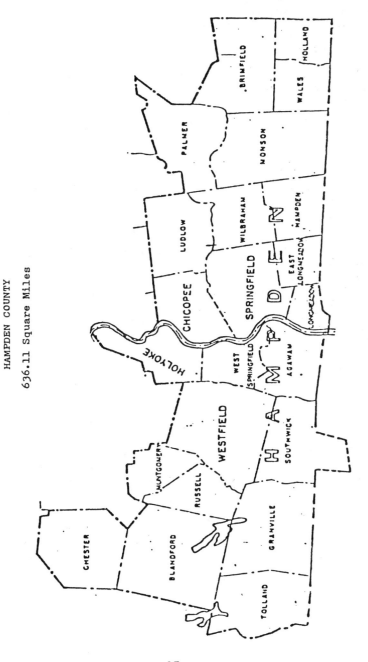

The Massachusetts Parole Board is the sole releasing agent of inmates in the Commonwealth. Parole eligibility has been established by the Board at one-half of the total aggregate sentence or two years, whichever is the shorter. In the case of motivated individuals, there is an avenue for earlier release under a contract approved by the Parole Board, the institution, and the inmate. This program is referred to as the Mutual Agreement Program. Under this program, the inmate may negotiate for an earlier release date, provided the inmate has successfully completed a number of specific programs as called for in the contract.

Every effort is made to separate the Jail and House of Correction inmates through the utilization of separate cell blocks. The present racial breakdown of the facility is as follows: 50 percent White, 33 percent Black, and 17 percent Hispanic (Puerto Rican).

In July, 1981 the inmate population was 345, approximately 89 inmates over capacity. (See Inmate Population Graph.) All females were transferred to the state institution for women at Farmingham to provide more space. Females have counselors from Hampden County Corrections going to the women's reformatory for the purpose of maintaing a pre-release program in preparation for their release to Hampden County.

Hampden County Correctional Programs

As was the case with the previously described case study in Oregon, we find a similar experience in Massachusetts. What will be described is a dynamic program offering multiple services for inmates and a sheriff and staff that have created a model corrections program in times of diminishing revenues. (Diminishing revenues in the state of Massachusetts are the result of the recently passed Proposition 2 1/2.) New programs are being implemented and very little in the way of human services is being sacrificed.

FIGURE 12

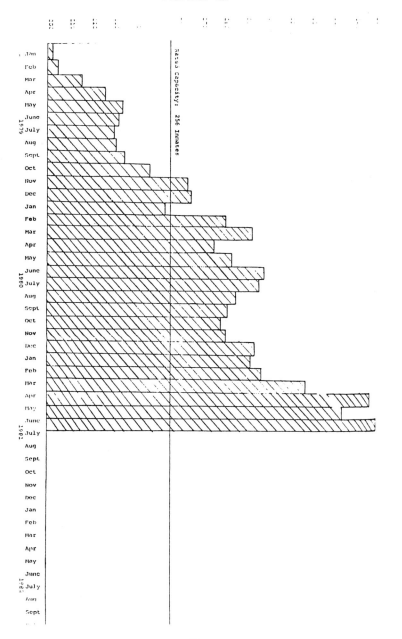

Much of the following was written by the staff of the jail and edited by this author.

Correctional Philosophy

For approximately a century, the Hampden County House of Correction provided the community with a warehouse that isolated the community and the convicted offenders from each other. Similar to other county correctional facilities across the nation, the Hampden County Jail and House of Correction represented the worst of the correctional system and the epitome of the debilitating effect of incarceration. Typical of most county facilities, the population it served was relatively untouched by human service programs or outside community support. A basic feeling of neglect and detachment was evident. Monies were not available for additional programs, renovations or maintenance of the physical plant. Updating staff effectiveness through training and modernization of an antiquated facility was out of the question. In almost every sense, the institution was to function as a human warehouse. Concern was for lock-up inmates and security, rather than for the gradual easement and reintegration to the community for the offender population.

The whole approach toward bringing rehabilitation programs into the Hampden County House of Correction begain in 1962 with the election of former Sheriff John G. Curley. In 1974, his rather impoverished programs were revitalized and new directions were taken in rehabilitation and reintegration concepts. Present Sheriff, Michael J. Ashe, Jr., an M.S.W. from Boston College, was overwhelmingly elected by campaigning on a treatment, rather than a security, problem. Since January of 1975, we have seen the establishment of a Classification Board to screen inmates for such programs as work release, furloughs, education and vocational skill training. The original purpose of the facility was outlined in the Annotated Laws of Massachusetts, Chapter 126, Section 8, which states that each county shall provide a house of correction, suitably and efficiently ventilated with convenient yards, workshops, and other suitable accommodations adjoining or appurtenant thereto, for the safekeeping, correction, government and employment of offenders legally committed thereto by the courts of the Commonwealth or Magistrates of the United States. In recent times, the purpose has expanded to include a focus on rehabilitation of its residents to the point where they can become integrated and contributing citizens. Preparing the individual to become successful in the community makes "good sense" when weighed against high recidivism rates and taxpayer burdens. The often quoted figures state that seven out of ten persons who have been incarcerated will be reincarcerated within seven years. The cost of maintaining the living arrangement of one inmate can cost between $12,000 and $15,000 per year. Any attempt to reduce such seemingly unpalatable statistics should be encouraged.

An integral component of this delivery system is a strong reliance on community based corrections. The Hampden County Correctional Facility, by virtue of its physical location, is central to the community it serves. As such, it presently has the potential to implement a total scope of services that includes allowing the incarcerated offender ultimately to prepare himself for and to support himself in the community, and that enables the community to be prepared for and supportive of the incarcerated offender's return. It is the intent of community based corrections to address these concerns of the correctional system and to counteract the depersonalizing effects of the correctional facility (dependency, isolation, inmate subculture, regimentation and dehumanization).

The typical correctional experience described above is to place offenders in an artificial environment which requires the learning of societal skills which are contrary to those necessary to sustain oneself in the community. The rehabilitative/reintegrative concept, advocated and proposed in a structured program to serve state sentenced inmates by this correctional facility, has addressed these problems.

Inmates at the Hampden County House of Correction have a wide variety of academic, personal and vocational needs that must be analyzed and fulfilled before effective, independent functioning can take place in the community. Clearly, there exists a profound lack of information available to the secluded inmate during his/her incarceration. In most cases, poor vocational choices or the lack of choice have preceded each sentenced individual. Everyone would agree that such limited choices will continue to be the "rule" unless greater opportunities begin to exist. Couple this with the fact that between 2,500 to 3,000 persons per year pass through the facility in various capacities. It is estimated that half, or above that number, of these individuals are released without definite employment prospects in the community.

The typical client/inmate has no significant work history, little work experience and few, if any, vocational options from which he/she can choose. The lack of marketable job skills and career objectives complicates matters. Over one-half of these individuals and families either receive unemployment payments or another form of public assistance (welfare) at the time of incarceration. Most client/inmates have not completed high school. The average grade level is eighth grade and the functional level is sixth grade. At any one time, demographic breakdowns reflect the following approximations: 45-50 percent Caucasians, 25-30 percent Hispanic, and 25-30 percent Black. Age statistics reflect the following: 50 percent between the ages of 17-25, 30 percent between the ages of 26-35, and 20 percent between the ages of 36 and above.

Although the preceding data are suggestive of factors leading to incarceration, experience has demonstrated that the mere provision of employment upon release does not ensure success. Emotional health, personal awareness, family relationships and other "deeply" rooted lifestyle patterns are immeasurably important. Unrealistic self-images, drug and/or alcohol dependence, etc. are other factors which may affect an individual's ability to be a productive member of society.

Since January, 1975, Sheriff Ashe and the staff of the House of Correction have been addressing the complex issues involved in the daily operation of a county correctional facility. They are keenly aware of the continuing controversy among professionals, academics, and various segments of the community regarding the purposes and the goals and methods of a correctional facility. It is the opinion of the institution's representatives that a clearly defined consensus regarding goals and objectives will not be explicit within the foreseeable future and that the institution is responsible for providing leadership in this area for Hampden County.

It has thus been concluded that in order to enhance public safety within Hampden County, the institution must blend a well-conceived and conscientious security plan with a comprehensive and structured human service delivery system. In the short run, the public safety goal must be achieved through bricks, mortor, bars and a trained security staff. In the long run, it is the belief and experience of this administration that public safety is enhanced through a comprehensive series of thoroughly structured, properly administered and purposeful human service programs.

To this end, the administration has developed a human service delivery system which attempts to maximize the positive impact of community resources. The programs which comprise the system at the Hampden County House of Correction are: Decisional Training (Thresholds), Jail Awareness for Juveniles, Alcoholics Anonymous, Bible Study (English and Spanish), Educational Programs (G.E.D. and college level), Basic remedial Education, English as a Second Language (ESL), Pre-Employment Training Program, After-care Followup Services, Vocational Skills Training (five occupational areas), Spanish Cultural Program, Pre-Release Center, cooperative relationships with out-of-town supportive service agencies, counseling services, and institutional work assignments. Although the entrance criteria for each program or activity may differ, participation is voluntary. Where it was once the case that inmates spent the majority of time confined to cells, an individual can now engage in human service activities and maintain a situation outside the cell for the majority of their time.

As part of the intake and classification process, inmates and counselors formulate a plan of activities which include specific goals within specific times. These goals and times vary according to length of sentence and interests.

It should be noted that the medical services department received accreditation by the American Medical Association and that the Pre-Release Program was recently accredited by the American Correctional Association. Also, a classification system and classification board have been established which reviews inmates' progress continually throughout their incarceration.

Security personnel have developed and implemented a policy and procedures manual, which clearly informs inmates of (a) the penalties for committing infractions and (b) explanation about their right to have their actions reviewed with the right to appeal any decision which is made concerning their alleged infraction.

Description of Programs

The Hampden County Jail and House of Correction is a diversified 256 bed facility, serving sentenced and pre-trial inmates within two major cell blocks and one dormitory, and a pre-release center.

Over the past several years a number of challenges have occurred to the facility administrators:

1. An ever increasing daily population;

2. A severe reduction in the age of the client population; and

3. An increase in the average sentence which is being handed down in the District and Superior Courts.

Given these and previously existing needs, the following programs have been instituted:

Skills Training Program

The Vocation Training Center is a school within the institution. It started as an arm of the Hampden District Regional Skill Center in Springfield. The Center is located in a previously unused but now renovated portion of the jail.

Opened in April, 1976 with a grant from the Massachusetts Department of Education, the Vocational Training Center functions in three separate areas:

1. The first area is a machine and welding shop equipped with engine lathes, drill presses, a bridgeport, a miller, a grinder, and welding booths. Inmates interested in manufacturing and related fields are trained in this area;

2. The second area is divided into four classrooms where inmates are instructed in

clerical skills, basic education, graphic arts, and electronics; and

3. In the third area culinary arts are taught to inmates who work in the jail's kitchen.

On October 1, 1978 the jail's Vocational Training Center became a training agency itself and thus qualified for Comprehensive Employment Training Act funds each year. The time of actual training in the program varies from twelve to eighteen weeks.

Adult Basic Education/Special Needs/ G.E.D. Preparation

Any sentenced inmate may earn a Massachusetts High School Equivalency Certificate while he or she is sentenced. Classes are held mornings, Monday through Friday from 9:00 A.M. to 11:00 A.M., and Monday through Friday afternoons from 1:00 P.M. to 3:00 P.M. Regular attendance is mandatory in order to insure proper study patterns. When an inmate enters the education program, a diagnostic test is administered to evaluate skill levels. After the test is scored, the student is placed in a program pertaining to his or her skill level. A cut-off grade level of fifth grade determines the need for special services. The special needs student is worked with on a one-to-one basis and through small group instruction. With some exceptions, the program uses self-paced programmed instruction booklets which provide immediate feedback on skills' mastery. The G.E.D. test is administered in the educational area every six weeks for all the students who have completed the program.

Pre-Employment Training Program

The Pre-Employment Training Program exposes the soon-to-be-released inmates (prior to work release, parole, or final discharge) to the nature, responsibilities and opportunities of living and working in the community. Basically an orientation program, the PETP offers the inmate five weeks of study in the areas of personality and self concept (one week), the family (one week), the community (one week), and employment (two weeks). Over fifty community resource people from business, government and community organizations discuss topics including: values, personality and temperment; response vs. manipulation; decisional training; human relations; family responsibilities; planned parenthood; housing; government and politics; budgeting the paycheck; banking services; credit; insurance; manpower needs in the county; preparing the job application; job interview process; mannerisms and appearance for seeking a job; how to find and keep a job; human relations on the job; vocational and educational opportunities; vocational interest; self concept and behavior; where to seek help in the community; recreational and leisure time; and others. Exposure to community resources and increased acceptance of the ex-offender by these resources increases the potential of a successful reintegration of clients into the community.

During the program, participants are evaluated on attendance, participation, and response to counseling sessions. Those successfully completing the program are given certificates of accomplishment and, when possible, honored at "graduation" ceremonies in the community. For most of the inmates, completing PETP marks the first time they have successfully finished a structured program.

Alcoholics Anonymous

This program meets on Sunday evenings at Hampden County Jail and House of Correction. The objectives and goals of the program are the same as any AA program. In order for an inmate to participate in this program, arrangements must be made with a caseworker.

Decisional Training

A twelve-week program consisting of individual and group counseling focuses on the process of goal setting and decision making. Volunteers from the community operate the program by assisting offenders affirm their worth as individuals. Volunteers help these men and women think about themselves in new, more positive ways.

Bible Study Program

This program is run by volunteers two evenings a week from 6:30 P.M. to 8:00 P.M.

The Hampden County Pre-Release Center

The Pre-Release Center of the Hampden County Jail and House of Correction is a residential facility designed to deinstitutionalize selected inmates prioir to their release to the community. PRC residents hold jobs, attend schools (and sometimes colleges), participate in job training programs outside the institution and return to the Pre-Release Center at night. The PRC experience lessens the negative impact of the institution and provides a very essential orientation in a setting close to the world the inmate will confront when he is released.

Located on the second and third floors of what was formerly the sheriff's residence, the PRC customarily houses fifteen to twenty-five residents. It functions with a staff of nine.

The objectives and accomplishments of the PRC are consistent with the enlightened view of corrections which holds that recidivism can be reduced by using practical methods to address achieveable corrections' objectives, and by establishing and cultivating the bonds between the institution and the community.

Advisory Council

Currently, Sheriff Ashe has instituted an advisory council so that community experts can provide advice on the operation of the facility. It also demonstrates a sound political strategy for involving citizens as advocates for the institution's needs.

The Advisory Board consists of ten members, each appointed by the sheriff for a term of one year. Representatives of the legal, medical, educatiqnal, recreational, business, construction, and religious communities are members of the Council, as well as the different ethnic minority groups which make up the inmate population.

All Advisory Board members undergo a two-day training session in which they are acquainted with the total operation of the Hampden County Jail and House of Correction. The members must also agree to meet at least six times yearly to offer recommendations directly to the sheriff on how to upgrade present conditions. The sheriff appoints the chairman of the council but the sheriff cannot remove the chairman without five votes of confirmation by the members of the Council. In December of every year, the Council is requested to make a final report of their activities and recommendations to the citizens of Hampden County. The sheriff serves as an ex-officio member of this Council.

Seven working committees develop program plans for the jail. These committees consist of:

o   Medical
o   Educational
o   Building
o   Recreational
o   Business
o   Legal
o   Religion

On the last weekend of every January, the sheriff and his staff provide a sixteen-hour, two-day training program for all Committee members. This program is designed to give all Committee members insight into the correctional institution they will be dealing with for the next year.

Correctional Accomplishments

Below are a list of accomplishments that Sheriff Ashe has completed since 1974, his first term in office.

Human Services

--Established the position of Director of Human Services with a rank equivalent to that of deputy administrator.

--Hired a full-time Director of Education to improve and expand educational services.

--Established a Pre-Employment Training Program as an element of the human services program.

--Established a job development placement component which spearheaded the eventual development of the Criminal Justice Review Committee to service all criminal justice clients in Hampden County.

--Expanded the furlough program and placed an individual directly in charge of the program; established a board to determine policy for the program and to select inmate participants.

--Established institutional skills training program in cooperation with the local CETA Skills Center ($110,000 grant).

--Established a Pre-Release Center to facilitate reintegration of the inmate population into the community. (To prepare inmates for transition to the outside world.)

--Established an After-Care Program to provide after-care services, in cooperation with the State Welfare Department, to the released population within Hampden County (made possible with United Way grant and Title XX money).

--Established a casework system to provide more effective services to the i nmate population and counter the warehouse syndrome.

--Established a Remedial Reading Program.

Physical Plant

--Completely renovated the femal section of the institution ($100,000 federal revenue-sharing money).

--Converted a garage and coal bin into the Skills Training Center (a jail, staff, and inmate assisted program).

--Renovated the West Bock area to separate the pre-trial and sentenced population ($300,000 federal revenue-sharing money).

--Remodeled and equipped the kitchen area (with staff and inmate help) and appointed a supervisor to improve the food services system.

--Converted the chapel and a storage area into a multi-service unit for education, pre-employment, training programs and a library.

--Secured $1,800,000 in federal revenue-sharing funds to renovate major areas of the institution.

--Secured $196,000 from the Economic Development Administration for new windows, a parking lot, a kitchen in the West Block, and renovation of the isolation unit.

Administration

--Established an Administration/Finance Department.

--Established the position of Personnel Director to work in the areas of personnel and labor relations.

--Established the position of Director of Business Office to operate and plan more efficiently for future needs of the institution.

--Established a Classification Department to better provide information to the institution for both security and human services needs.

--Established a Medical Department to provide a higher level and wider range of medical services and, in July, 1979, received AMA accreditation.

--Contracted with the Crime and Justice Foundation, Inc. of Boston to manage a self-evaluation of the facility and to comply with state and national accreditation standards. (Made possible with a local Dexter Fund grant.)

--Assigned an accreditation team to organize and enhance the effort for national accreditation at the institution. In addition, the National Institute for Corrections has provided technical assistance to achieve this goal.

--Obtained a $500,000 CETA public service employment grant to allow one institution staff to address the action plan for development and implementation of standards.

--Entered into agreement with the Massachusetts Criminal Justice Training Academy to provide a minimum of 120 hours of basic corrections training for all staff members.

A clear reflection of the underlying mission of the corrections program in Hampden County is provided by the Decisional Training Program, staffed mainly by volunteers from the community.

This year marks the program's five-year anniversary. It is worthwhile to inventory the benefits of the program to inmate and community alike, to examine areas of growth in the program, and to project the future.

The Decisional Training Program is unique in that it is a community based volunteer program aimed at inmates within the correctional institution. It benefits not only the inmates, and thus the community in which they live, but the volunteers themselves. They gain self worth and self confidence by being involved in a program designed to help others, and they may incorporate the learning acquired into their own lives. Their work is an extension of the counseling services already available to the inmate population. This does not mean just an increase in the quantity of counseling hours available, but an increase in quality of counseling services also. The quality of the program is insured by the thorough training of each volunteer.

Individuals who lack the knowledge and abilities necessary to conform to societal standards will only retain those behaviors which have been helpful in their past ability to survive. It is particularly important that these individuals become aware of these unproductive behaviors. Many offenders have not acquired societal skills from their families or our public institutions of learning. The problem then in attempting to prepare these offenders for community involvement is pragmatically one of remediation.

The Decisional Training Program attempts to correct this problem by assisting offenders to alter their behaviors. Program success can be measured in terms of number of persons who do not return to jail. By the same token, if only one decision a person makes is more effective and benefical toward a desired outcome, the training has left a permanent mark. In the past five years of service to Hampden County, the staff of Decisional Training has amassed over 32,000 volunteer hours of service. Also, over 250 male and female offenders have been participants in training weekends.

Individual counselors interested in participating in the Decisional Trainiung Program are screened by the volunteer staff and asked to attend the training weekend, which includes nearly twenty hours of instruction. They attend at their own expense and pay a $20 fee to be trained. Volunteers include housewives, lawyers, students, business persons; in short, all kinds of people with concern for their community and those persons who live in it. The volunteers give service to the community and are rewarded by the positive feelings attached to assisting another human being resolve and clarify life problems. The entire process makes for an extremely worthwhile relationship for both the volunteer and the inmate.

Counselors attend in-service training seminars in order to lend support to one another and discuss individual techniques which have proved worthwhile or problematic. These sessions also become a forum to discuss internal and external concerns which effect the entire program. A cycle manager is responsible for coordinating these meetings and maintaining a cooperative relationship with jail officials. Throughout each twelve-week cycle, the cycle manager and jail staff discuss matters of mutual concern.

As a result of this program, inmates begin to solve problems responsibly. Volunteers affirm the inmates' worth as individuals and enlarge their character and self esteem. In such manner, participants begin to think more positively and place their future and environment in absolute perspective. Situational factors are recognized as a true component of a good decision making process. By making their own decisions based upon boundaries, odds, risks and desirability of goal attainment, individuals now take more control over their lives.

Because the counselor is a volunteer, he/she can take liberties that the correctional staff at the jail cannot. The volunteer can ask questions, point out inconsistencies, gather data, push for the truth. The inmate realizes this unique role and becomes more willing to volunteer information which otherwise would be hidden beneath a facade created to survive in the jail setting. The counselor is under no obligation to anyone and is there only because he/she cares. This important program serves as an extension of the existing counseling services at the Hampden County House of Correction. The cost of staffing such a program with paid positions would be prohibitive.

Sheriff Ashe takes security at his facility very seriously, but programs appear to take a priority. In sum, as the above volunteer program's philosophy clearly indicates, offender resocialization predominates as the major theme within this jail. Security usually attempts to work closely with human service programs, thus lessening the treatment-custody conflict which is so pervasive in corrections today.*

The deputy superintendent or director of all human service programs is Jay Ashe, who has an M.S.W. degree and came to the jail after years of experience as a social worker in residential programs for juvenile delinquents.

Jay Ashe not only adminstrates and coordinates all human service programs, he is very active in gaining community, state and federal resources for inmate programs. Much of the funding available to the facility is the direct result of Sheriff Ashe's and Jay Ashe's community contacts.

Jail Organization

The following charts illustrate the organization's personnel structure and financial situation.

Figure 13
Hampden County Jail Personnel

I. Security (uniform) - 87   1 Major (Asst. Deputy Administrator)
                               7 Captains
                              13 Lieutenants
                               8 Senior Correctional Officers
                              58 Correctional Officers

II. Pre-Release - 9   1 Project Director
                              1 Senior Correctional Counselor
                              3 Correctional Counselors
                              1 Secretary/Correctional Aide
                              2 Correctional Aides
                              1 Part-time Aide

* It must be noted that Deputy Superintendent Nick Fiorentino, who has the correctional officers under his administration, is an attorney with a J.D. degree. His concern with abiding by legal standards in dealing with inmates and his support for human services has done much to ease custody-treatment tensions.

III.	After-care Services -4	1 3	Manager After-care Counselors
IV.	Skills Center -6	3 3	Instructors Aides
V.	Human Services - 11	1 1 1 1 2 2 1 2	Director Director of Classification Manager Pre-Trial and Library Services Vocational Guidance Coordinator Correctional Officer Counselors Counselors Educational Aide/Counselor Special Education Teachers
VI.	Food Services -4	1 1 2	Director of Food Services Senior Steward Prison Chefs
VII.	Medical - 5	1 1 1 1 1	Director of Medical Department Medical Coordinator Medical Correctional Officer Nurse Junior Clerk
VIII.	Chaplains - 2	1 1	Protestant (part-time) Roman Catholic (part-time)

IX.	Administration - 13	1
		1
		1
		
		1
		
		1
		1
		1
		1
		1
		3
		1
			Sheriff
			Deputy Administrator (Operations)
			Deputy Administrator (Human
			  Services)
			Asst. Deputy Administrator
			  (Finance)
			Administrative Aide
			Personnel Manager
			Business Office Manager
			Head Administrative Clerk
			Principle Clerk
			Junior Clerks
			Secretary

	Total	143	Employees

Appropriations

The Hampden County correctional facility received the following county appropriation for FY 7/1/78 to 6/30/79:

Table 13
County Appropriation for
Jail and House of Correction

Appropriation	$1,985,323.66
Emergency Loan	-0-
Transfer from Reserve Fund 28	1,495.40
Transfer from Reserve Fund 28A	35,989.54
Transfer from Reserve Fund 28D	-0-
Transfer from Reserve Fund 28F	24,500.00
Expenditures	2,206,866.17
Reserved Balance	15,649.00
Unexpected Balance	45,293.43

For FY 7/1/79 to 6/30/80, the appropriation was as follows:

Table 14
County Appropriation for
Jail and House of Correction

Appropriation	$2,063,358.87
Supplemental Budget	9,024.62
Transfer from Reserve Fund 28	3,850.10
Transfer from Reserve Fund 28F	343,000.00
Expenditures	2,372,400.47
Reserved Balance	-0-
Unexpected Balance	46,833.12

The 1981-1982 expenditures are expected to increase approximately 9.3 percent, while the projected increase in population is estimated to be 16 percent. Added to the above 1979-80 appropriation figure, the jail received $600,000 for renovations to the physical plant. Out of federal reveune sharing, the jail received from the county commissioners 1.8 million dollars over a three-year period for construction renovation of the jail. This appropriation was divided over a three year period as follows:

Table 15
Federal Revenue Sharing Funds

Jail Reserve	1976-77, Code 709	-	$600,000
Jail Reserve	1978-79, Remodeling	-	$600,000
Jail Reserve	1979-80, Code 709	-	$600,000

Due to the age of the correctional facility, coupled with the tremendous increases in inmate population over the last several years, the sheriff has requested the following funds from the state legislature for new construction and renovation. This request was in addition to the 1.8 million dollars previously received by the county from federal revenue sharing funds. The following statement was taken from a news editorial in which Sheriff Ashe was utilizing media sources to gain public support for state funding in order to complete the institution's renovation and new construction.

> Sheriff Ashe calls our attention to the Hampden County State Representative delegation which spoke with Speaker McGee and Governor King about the York Street Jail's request for 4.5 million dollars. Three quarters of that money would be used for new construction and one quarter for jail renovation. If York Street were to receive the necessary funds 102 new bed spaces would be added to the institution. We hope you will urge your legislators and the Governor to build the necessary jails and free up the money necessary to improve the existing ones.

One of the innovative strategies utilized by all county correctional facilities in Massachusetts was the agreement to house sentenced inmates in the jail instead of having them sent to a state correctional institution. This agreement between the State Department of Corrections and the county sheriffs serves two mutiple purposes. First, it helps to alleviate overcrowding in the state penal system, a serious problem in Massachusetts. Second, it provides state reimbursements to county jails at the rate of $10,000 per inmate per year. As the following memorandum illustrates, Hampden County will receive $140,000 in FY 1982 for keeping fourteen state-sentenced offenders in their facility. This funding will assist the human services program at the jail. In light of the severe financial revenue reductions with the passage of proposition 2 1/2, these reimbursement dollars are extremely important.

O J. HOLWAY
·y Commissioner

The Commonwealth of Massachusetts

Department of Correction

Leverett Saltonstall Building, Government Center

100 Cambridge Street, Boston 02202

July 27, 1981

TO: Representative Charles F. Flaherty, Jr.
        Chairman, Committee on Counties

FROM: David J. Holway, Deputy Commissioner

RE: Expected DOC Funds to Counties

        The following is a list of what counties are to receive state
reimbursements for services rendered to the department from 4/1/81
thru 6/30/81:

Barnstable	3,655.43
Berkshire	1,445.49
Bristol	14,885.82
Essex	8,881.46
Franklin	2,307.23
Hampden	13,662.71
Hampshire	13,940.69
Middlesex	20,876.29
Norfolk	1,181.41
Plymouth	3,419.15
Suffolk	15,219.40
Worcester	12,189.42

        As you know, the department has received $500,000. to reimburse
the counties for FY82. The department estimates that we will average
approximately 50 state inmates for the year. The department intends to
place the majority of these at institutions that have available bed
space and offer services to pre-release inmates. I expect that the
following is a fairly accurate estimate of where the FY82 funds will
be spent:

Berkshire	10,000
Bristol	20,000
Essex	60,000
Franklin	30,000
Hampden	140,000
Hampshire	180,000
Norfolk	10,000
Plymouth	20,000
Worcester	20,000

107

Representative Charles F. Flaherty, Jr.
Page 2
July 27, 1981

It should be noted that the allocations to Hampden, Hampshire and Essex are based upon the assumption that they will continue to be able to provide the excellent reintergration and training services currently available.

The Hampden figure is contingent upon the funding of Item 28G (Community Intergration for State Inmate Program) at $115,000. The people employed by these funds will be providing services not only to state inmates but to the over 300 county inmates as well. I would like to point out that your committee last year appropriated $40,000. in item 28G for the program with the agreement that the department would reimburse the county $60,000. I am happy to report that the county will receive a total of $63,726 for FY81 for the program plus the #13,662.71 outlined earlier for a total of $77,388 for FY81.

County Revenues

In Massachusetts there are three general representative bodies that review and make decisions for county budgets: (1) County commissioners; (2) County advisory boards; and (3) State Committee on Counties, which is a committee of the state legislature and which recommends budgets to the entire state legislature. Final signature of all county budgets is made by the governor.

The Legislative Process for County Budget

Step 1 Submission of departmental budgets to County Commissioner's Office. All budgets are on standard forms issued by the State.

Step 2 Commissioners' hearings on the departmental budgets. Department chiefs of large departments are called in to explain budget. (Members of the County Advisory Board may be present.)

Step 3 First vote by Commissioners. Budget sent to County Advisory Board.

Step 4 Discussion of budget by County Advisory Board Executive Committee and/or full board membership. Recommendations for changes are voted upon, and these are returned to Commissioners.

Step 5 Final vote by Commissioners on budget which is then sent to County Advisory Board and State Committee on Counties.

Step 6 Final vote by Advisory Board - any two-third vote which opposed any item of Commissioner's budget is sent to State Committee on Counties.

Step 7 Public hearings by State Committee on Counties. (Joint Committee of House and Senate.)

Step 8 Committee research and deliberations - additions and cuts.

Step 9 Committee report (favorable) - considered first reading on House and Senate floors. Amendments can be made to budgets.

Step 10 Budget on House and Senate floors - second and third readings. If the House or Senate makes changes in committee report, and the other branch accepts, the changes are entered and sent to the Governor. However, if one branch makes changes which are not accepted by the other branch, a conference committee will be established to work out differences.

Step 11 Budget sent to governor for signature. He must accept or reject the total package, as he is unable to make line item changes.

Hampden County, as the following tax rate table clearly indicates, has experienced lowering tax rates for most of its cities and towns over a three-year period. Proposition 2 1/2 is the legislative summary of recent actions.

Table 17
Tax Rates of the Cities and Towns in Hampden County

Agawam	$ 48.50	$ 49.50	$ 48.50
Blandford	151.00	21.00	16.00
Brimfield	115.00	115.00	119.00
Chester	32.80	33.80	34.00
CHICOPEE	220.00	222.00	184.00
East Longmeadow	40.00	40.00	39.00
Granville	138.00	148.00	22.50
Hampden	48.00	33.50	35.00
Holland	170.00	149.00	21.70
HOLYOKE	166.00	166.00	102.00
Longmeadow	49.00	54.00	49.00
Ludlow	64.00	71.00	75.00
Monson	52.40	66.80	27.20
Montgomery	—	—	46.00
Palmer	27.50	35.50	32.00
Russell	43.00	137.00	130.00
Southwick	43.00	48.00	42.00
SPRINGFIELD	85.50	97.50	87.00
Tolland	40.00	77.00	42.00
Wales	91.00	38.00	38.00
West Springfield	45.50	51.00	49.50
WESTFIELD	74.00	70.00	65.00
Wilbraham	51.00	29.00	33.70

Proposition 2 1/2 is extremely complicated and the effects of this legislation on cities and counties is not clear at this time.

One explanation of the proposition's intent is best explained in the article on page 118 which details some major elements of the legislation. These particular mandates were legally contested by public employees who are members of various labor unions. In the same newspaper appeared the following account of the property tax increases in Massachusetts for 1980-81.

Supreme Judicial Court says Prop. 2½ is legal

By Alan Sheehan
Globe Staff

Proposition 2½, the taxpayers' response to increased property taxes and municipal spending, "was legally adopted" and the renter's deduction is constitutional, the Massachusetts Supreme Judicial Court declared yesterday.

The court, in a unanimous opinion written by Justice Herbert P. Wilkins, rejected a challenge brought by unions representing teachers, police officers, correctional officers and five taxpayers.

The plaintiffs contended that Proposition 2½ was not a proper subject of an initiative petition and that procedural requirements of the initiative authorized by the Constitution were not properly followed in the presentation to the voters.

The renter's deduction from taxable income of 50 percent of rent paid also was challenged as being unconstitutional.

The court held that "all the subjects included in Proposition 2½ relate directly or indirectly to the limitation of state and local taxation."

The court, therefore, dismissed the argument that "each of the substantive provisions of Proposition 2½ should have been presented separately."

"It is clear ... that an initiative measure may include more than one subject," the court said. "The constitutional requirement is only that those subjects be related."

The Massachusetts Teachers Assn. (MTA) further argued that the tax-cutting act violates state law because it does not apply uniformly throughout the state.

What the union was referring to was the section of the law which has special provisions concerning municipalities whose total taxes assessed in fiscal year 1979 were less than 2½ percent of the full and fair cash value of real and personal property.

"The law is not directed to specific cities and towns," the court held, in rejecting the challenge.

"It deals with property tax-reductions or limitations throughout the commonwealth, although in different degrees and in different ways, and in all instances is subject to local control."

The teachers' association attacked the section of the law regarding elimination of fiscal autonomy of school committees because the powers of the courts are improperly implicated in the changes wrought by the law.

"If, as is the case, the fiscal autonomy of school committees may be abolished by an initiative measure, judicial enforcement of fiscal autonomy may also be abolished," the court said. "The abolition of the judicial remedy has only an incidental effect on the power of the courts."

"Adoption of a contrary view should suggest that the initiative process could not make any change in any law that was enforceable in the courts, that is, virtually any change in the law at all," Wilkins said in his 50-page opinion.

The plaintiffs also challenged the summary of the law that was drafted by Atty. Gen. Francis X. Bellotti and placed on the ballot.

The court found that the section of the summary dealing with fiscal autonomy was "a concise and fair summary of the consequences of Proposition 2½ in relation to the fiscal autonomy of local and regional school committees. To be sure, the summary was brief in this respect. But is was fair and correct."

Considering what the court termed "a clear error," the court said the summary erroneously stated to voters that they ought to consider their then current tax rate in relation to the proposed ... tax ceiling and not the tax rate for the fiscal year 1979 to which the proposed act actually applied in cases where that rate was less than two and one-half percent."

The court ruled that "in the entire scheme of Proposition 2½ and the attorney general's summary, the error, although unfortunate, was minor and not significantly misleading."

The court noted that proponents of the act intended to eliminate final and binding arbitration for police officers and firefighters but in framing the proposal the wrong section of the law was used.

This error resulted in a "perfecting change," which the International Brotherhood of Police Officers alleged is not constitutionally permissible.

The court, however, upheld the attorney general's opinion that the perfecting change met the requirements of the law.

The court found that the challenges to the renter's deduction — that it violated the constitutional standard of equal protection — had no merit.

"The renter's deduction tends to reduce the disparate treatment of the home owner and home renter in the operation of the income tax law," the court ruled.

The court, in effect, upheld a 70-page decision rendered April 1 by Judge William G. Young.

And, as in that opinion, the court yesterday was reviewing the law basically on "technical aspects of how the ballot questions were adopted" and not whether Proposition 2½ interfered unconstitutionally with union contracts.

Mass. property taxes reported up

Associated Press

Property taxes in Massachusetts, which Gov. Edward J. King sought to cut by $500 million, rose by $345 million – 11.5 percent – in fiscal 1981, it was reported yesterday.

The analysis by the Massachusetts Taxpayers Foundation put the levy – the amount cities and towns raise from real and personal property taxes – at $3.35 billion. This is the principal source of revenue for the 351 cities and towns, which spent $5.29 billion in the year that ended June 30.

The Taxpayers Foundation said the increase was the largest since 1977 and followed a 1 percent decline in 1980. The increase was attributed to inflation, a decline in state aid, higher state and county assessments and depleted reserves, which helped lower the 1980 levy.

The average tax rate was $61.65 per $1000 in valuation, which the foundation claimed was based on a 61 percent assessment ratio. They said the average full valuation tax rate would have been $37.90.

The foundation declared that the 4 percent cap imposed on municipal spending by King and the Legislature was unsuccessful because it had been too often overridden.

"Expenditures covered by the law increased by more than 4 percent in 242 communities," the analysis revealed.

The Taxpayers Foundation is an influential private business-supported organization that monitors government spending at the state and local levels.

In fiscal 1981 – the same year voters approved tax-cutting Proposition 2½ – the organization noted that tax rates were increased in 227 communities.

The analysis said the rate remained the same in 17 communities and declined in 107 communities, "with revaluations probably accounting for the lower rates in those communities."

The analysis showed comparative data on 1980 and 1981 tax rates. The foundation reported that the average assessment in Boston is 36 percent of total value. The 1981 tax rate was $272.70 and if property were at 100 percent assessment, the tax rate would have been $99, far above the state average, the foundation said.

The organization listed 77 communities with 100 percent valuations. At the low end of the spectrum, with data unavailable from a few communities, the assessments in West Tisbury (on Martha's Vineyard) and Dunstable represented only 9 percent of valuations. Other low ratios included Uxbridge, 11 percent; Billerica and Carver were 12 percent, Clinton, Methuen, Millbury and Shirley, 13 percent; Boxford and Dracut at 14 percent.

Direct Effect of Proposition 2 1/2
on Hampden County

The county, as a direct outcome of Proposition 2 1/2, must begin to make fiscal cuts in FY 1981 in order to comply with the property tax mandates of this new law. The article from the Springfield Daily News, on page 121 provides a clear analysis for the task of cutting back for Hampden County officials. Note that with employee pay raises, together with inflation factors, the County has been asked by the state legislature Committee on Counties to cut $407,139 from this year's (1981) budget.

The table on page 122 illustrates the fiscal circumstances Hampden County is currently experiencing as a result of a capping of property tax assessment for FY 1981. Although the 1981 assessment indicates an increase from 1980's, it falls far below the funds needed to operate county government. The cuts that have been made appera to be minimal when compared to a total FY 1981 budget of $9,903,363. However, one must take into account increases in expenditures as well as inflation which normally would have added to the revenue sources.

In summary, the state of Massachusetts and Hampden County area in for some tough fiscal times. This is not to say that both state and county have not already experienced severe fiscal constraints, but they will face an even greater decrease in revenue producing taxes which will put a great strain on all levels of government. Innovative management strategies for the continued provision of public services are of utmost importance.

The Hampden County Sheriff and his total organization are utilizing multiple political, managerial, and fiscal strategies in order to preserve their programs.

114

justice committee which does make funding
dations. Also, Sheriff Ashe has a good working
ship with other sheriffs in Massachusetts, and together
ve attempted to lobby for state funds for county
ons.

ndards are a very important part of the sheriff's
ent program. As pointed out previously, the pre-release
and the medical services programs have received A.C.A.
ation. Under Nick Fiorentino, Deputy Superintendent for
ns, a complete policy manual outlining job descriptions
 assignments for security and custody staff has been
d. Gary King, Director of Classification, along with
 has implemented an inmate classification system that is
l throughout the period of an inmate's incarceration.
 are checked for progress and are reclassified, if
ate, upon request. Overall, it appears that Sheriff Ashe
ized the challenge of meeting national jail standards as a
to operate his organization in a manner that is in
ce with constitutional practices.

es of the Community

r since Sheriff Ashe was elected in January, 1974, his
heme for attaining improvements for the jail's physical
nd the development and implementation of reintegration
 for inmates has been community involvement. Sheriff Ashe
ackground in human services, a master's degree in social
nd because of his educational and professional experience
becoming sheriff, he has the unique ability to understand
in the community. Although being a sheriff is very
al, he well understands that working together with the
ty is essential if support for his overall mission is to be
ished. One of the factors that appears to have become an
ve tool in order to gain community support for programs has
 opening up of the institution for public scrutiny. The
 is a strong advocate of sharing his jail operational
s with elected officials as well as community groups. He
rovides tours of the facility to people in positions of
al power and claims to bring the media in on such
ns. His use of the media, especially newspapers, is
ed by the numerous articles that are kept in a scrapbook.
early understands the political climate of the city, county
e state, and together with his political skills has
ed solid community support for the type of offender
s he has instituted. He often appears on local radio and
ion programs to inform the public of what he is doing for
ates, and uses such media opportunities to educate citizens
he obstacles that his jail is experiencing while trying to
 a decent and secure environment in which to operate the
y's programs:

118

County Commissioners Discuss Budget Cuts

Daily News 7/22/81

The Hampden County Commission met today to discuss making further cuts of more than $400,000 in its fiscal year 1982 budget.

It was learned Tuesday in Boston that the legislative Committee on Counties decided the county budget must be cut another $407,139 to stay within the 4 percent local assessment cap mandated by Proposition 2½ or $714,705 to be level funded with last year's budget total.

State Rep. Edward W. Connelly, R-Agawam, said it is the preference of legislators from Hampden County that the budget be funded at last year's local assessment of $7,689,150. However, Connelly said, the Committee on Counties will allow the county to cut either amount.

Officials of Hampden County and other counties in the state facing the same option must report their decision to the committee by the end of this week so that county budgets can be approved.

After today's meeting, the commissioners will meet with county advisory board members.

The Hampden County budget request as adopted by commissioners and the advisory board totals $9.9 million.

According to figures released by the Committee on Counties, this year's total budget request is $136,705 above the amount of money available last year. Added to that figure is $578,000 for salary increases for a total of $714,705 that will be needed to match last year's local assessment of $7,689,150.

But because the authorized assessment this year is $7,996,716, only $407,139 in cuts would be required to comply with the 4 percent local assessment cap.

Next year, legislative approval will not be necessary for county budgets.

115

Table 18
Hampden County Tax Assessment – 1981

Budget Request	$9,903,363
Last Year's Assessment	7,689,150
Revenue Sharing Funds	617,508
Estimated Receipts	1,160,000
TOTAL	$9,466,658
Estimated Free Cash	300,000
TOTAL	$9,766,658
Difference from Budget Request	$ 136,705
Funds for Salary Increases Voted this Year	578,000
Amount of Cuts Necessary for Level Assess	714,705
Proposition 2 1/2 Authorized Assessment	$7,996,716
Amount of Cuts Necessary under 2 1/2	407,139

Local, State and Federal Influences Effecting the Jail

Most of the publicity concerning Proposition 2 1/2 has come from the city of Boston, where layoffs of police, firemen, teachers and other public employees have occurred. Not much has been heard from smaller cities of the state; but as previously shown, Hampden County has had to cut over $400,000 from the 1981 county budget and more cuts will most likely be required for FY 1982. The total impact of Proposition 2 1/2 will not be known until late in 1982.

Obviously, federal funds have been significant to Hampden County correctional programs. Although the majority of funding comes from the county treasury, federal dollars for human services has been the impetus for many programs. In some cases, program costs have been picked up by the county under three-year matching grant formulas used by L.E.A.A. But, now the county cannnot take over funding of all implemented programs. It is interesting to note that Sheriff Ashe and his two deputy administrators are very astute in attaining needed funding for corrections programs. When it comes to the creation of resocialization programs for inmates,

Hampden County Corrections leaves no stone u... continually engaged in proposal writing, a... are consistently attempting to integrate the... those pre-existing in the community. The s... have excellent ties to community agencies, e... of job training and employment opportunity l... that where an avenue exists for integratinç... with other agencies' services, they will ... interests.

The overcrowding problem that has exis... years has yet to become a major problem rela... of services. However, the institution's p... considerably in the near future, resulting... overall operation. However, even with the ov... in the jail, the administration has profited... It must be emphasized that fourteen state-se... be serving their time in the jail at a... Corrections Department of $140,000 of which $1... county jail budget, and $25,000 is given to... general fund.

In addition to the $115,000, the jail r... the state for female offenders who are curre... Farmingham, a women's state reformatory. The... are being contracted from the state to the... facility is due to the fact that counselors f... services to the transferred female inmates at... as provide pre-release and after-care services... example of the cooperation between agencies at... government.

Even in times of fiscal adversity, the ad... Hampden County Sheriff's Department has found... costs in a diminishing fiscal situation... willingness to find solutions by contracting... agencies is well known.

The sheriff and his two administrato... relationship with elected officials. ... commissioners, along with the county advisory c... be supportive of the sheriff's attempts a... services to offenders incarcerated in the jai... important, the sheriff's relationship with ... delegation in the legislature, the legisla... Counties, the Governor as well as the Commissi... and other administrative people at the state... and profitable. It is not unusual for the sher... travel to the state capital to meet with ... officials. Sheriff Ashe is an appointed member...

In the last six years we have tried to take advantage of our newness plus the desire and the enthusiasm to do some positive things here and try to build some bridges between the county commissioners and the legislative body, and very much involve the media. Invite them in.

Sheriff Ashe claims that he uses a common sense approach in dealing with the community and elected officials. "It's really common sense, letting people know what your problems are." Perhaps his openness and willingness to let the community know just what the constraints are on his operation has been one of the strategies, that has proven to be most effective.

Planning for Budget Cutbacks

Many of the actual strategies for maintaining correctional programs have been discussed previously. A brief summary of the major managerial practices relating to productive use of scarce resources would be beneficial.

Perhaps the most important factor which has allowed for the maintenance of offender programs has been the high community profile which the sheriff and his staff maintain. As a direct result of this visibility, Sheriff Ashe has developed strong citizen support for his efforts to gain the necessary funds to operate county corrections. Obviously, there are other management practices he and his staff have used. They include:

1. Use of volunteers in some of the offender resocialization programs which saves needed dollars and provides staff at no cost to the jail;

2. An inmate classification system which results in better management of inmate supervision as well as avoiding duplication of services to inmates;

3. Systematic use of the media, both newspapers and television, in a pro-active way to sell the needs of the jail to the citizens of the county. Such utilization of the local media appears to be an effective tool to educate the public concerning the goals and objectives of the jail's programs:

4. The pro-active nature in which the sheriff and the two deputy superintendents consistently plan for methods of funding for the total jail operation. This pro-active approach in planning, although in the recent past, appears

to resemble "crisis planning" due to the decreases in revenue caused by Proposition 2 1/2, and appears to include the following elements:

a. Internal

1. Periodic staff analysis of forecasted needs, both in security and human services;

2. Consistent plans for renovation of the jail and alternative plans which provide needed options;

3. Involving staff in fiscal decisions in the areas of modifying personnel resources in order to prioritize program needs in times of diminishing fiscal restraints;

4. Movement of prisoners to various areas within the jail to make better use of space for offender programs. This includes mainly renovation of particular areas within the facility which had potential for added physical space, but were old and housed such things as a coal bin and boiler room.

b. External

1. Close ties to county and state elected and administive officials for the purpose of gaining political support for the jail;

2. Open house policy - frequent use of tours to educate public officials and citizens' groups;

3. Knowledge of funding opportunities at the county, state and federal level of government together with frequent contact with such funding sources;

4. Instituting an advisory board for the jail which consists of citizens from the professional and business community;

5. Frequent utilization of county agencies and employment opportunities for inmates in the work-release program and job skills program.

In summary, the Hampden County corrections program has for years been planning and implementing programs and gathering the necessary resources. Because of the pro-active stance of Sheriff Ashe and his staff, planning is an ongoing process that, even in the face of funding cuts, the jail operation will not suffer dramatically. This is not to say that the jail staff are not concerned with funding cutbacks, but rather that the agressive planning posture will be characteristic of the future as Ashe and others implement strategies to gain resources necessary to fulfill their program goals. As the sheriff stated when asked about his overall management style in this era of diminishing funds for public programs:

> We always watch things politically. Always seeing, working together. If I've brought anything to the institution, it's not my administrative ability, but working together with people to accomplish goals. It's awfully important to work positively.

Deputy Superintendent of Operations Fiorentino comments on the same issue:

> We feel that because we have developed this relationship both with the county commissioners and the county advisory board will allow us to continue these programs. They will pick it up (funding) . . . The strategy is to show them (county elected officials) that we are in fact operating the institution in accordance with state and federal guidelines and providing the county with a facility that is operating in a safe and secure setting for the inmates and the general population of Hampden County.

Sheriff Ashe, in formulating an institutional board of directors, has done so for many reasons. One of them is to integrate the jail with the business community. A direction which the sheriff feels is essential in these times of depleted governmental support:

> The place (jail) has been so isolated, so aloof from the community. The more you bring it out and the more you identify your problems and goals there is going to be more and more cooperation from business and industry.

Sheriff Ashe continued:

> I've got to get the board of directors involved — that's the first step. I have got to get labor and business involved — My second six years is to reach out into the community and in a much bigger and more indepth way.

121

The plan for managing with scarce resources appears to be one in which the pre-existing involvement of the community in support for the corrections program will be intensified. The attempted inclusion of labor and business in providing a portion of the needed funds for programs in the jail's human services area is a new strategy. It may be one that works if the sheriff can rally support from these private sector sources. Ashe's plan to use the board of directors may be a bit optimistic, but it is a relationship that must be nurtured if he is going to keep his organization's programs from diminishing:

> Now it is a case of holding on to what we have got. . . Now I've got to work much harder on the outside. The advisory board (board of directors) will give me some strong arms to get some money.

It is apparent that the first six-year term of the sheriff's tenure was spent in two major areas of organizational develpment. The first was reorganizing the jail staff; hiring new personnel and getting the human services programs instituted and operational. The second was Sheriff Ashe's development of wide-spread community and political support.

These next six years, if one can predict the future, will be devoted to attaining funding for the jail through attempting to maintain political support from elected officials in the county and state, as well as attempts to involve private sector business and labor to contribute some portion of money for the continuation of programs. There will be more emphasis put on external matters on the part of the sheriff and less involvement in the internal day-to-day operations of the organization. According to Ashe:

> The state legislature, that's the key. That's where the action is, that's where I get the resources I bring to the institution. No sense in me sitting here. That's the name of the game.

This observer is of the opinion that Sheriff Ashe will always keep abreast of the internal operations of the jail no matter how much time his external work will take. However, the sheriff has his administrators functioning quite well in their positions. Because the two deputy superintendents are professional administrators and work quite well together, the sheriff can devote more time externally on gaining the necessary resources from the private and public sectors.

The only weakness in the sheriff's strategy seems to be in the area of attempting to reduce the jail's population. It will be difficult to maintain the quality of inmate programs if the population of the facility increases. Overcrowding, which currently exists, will result in less effective delivery of human services. What, perhaps, is needed is a closer working relationship with judges for the purpose of finding alternatives to the use of the jail for sentenced offenders who do not need to be incarcerated, but could profit from alternative programs. This could result in keeping the jail population down as well as being a more cost effective plan for those sentenced by the courts.

Administration's View on Offenders

It should be apparent that the purpose of the programs provided by the Hampden County Jail is to offer offenders various opportunities to lead law-abiding and productive lives. To ensure that the human services programs are a major priority, both the sheriff and his two top administrators have attempted to professionalize the staff. In order to lessen the conflict between security staff and human services personnel — a conflict which always permeates correctional programs with a strong treatment emphasis — the human services and operations administrators work extremely close. Both groups see the human services programs as a major priority and security, as a goal to be operationalized around human services' purposes. Fiorentino comments:

> The human services staff has entered into an informal agreement with the security staff in that they realize the benefits derived from people being active (inmates). Jay (Human Resources Administrator) and his staff, because of the successes with it, keep refining it (informal agreement between custody and treatment staff).

Sheriff Ashe is of the belief that no inmate should be idle. All the programs appear to be based on the philosophy that while an offender is incarcerated, he or she should be provided opportunities and incentives to take advantage of the many programs offered in the jail.

> What I am trying to do is pay these guys (inmates) off with a challenge. We are trying to break some new ground in county corrections. Try and enhance the community corrections concept. We are big on standards and it is all tied to our original concept of professionalization.

On the overall program for inmates, the sheriff states the following:

123

Education and vocational training is our goal.
Get inmates back into the community. . . . Everybody
starts in our main block; they are assigned a
counselor; they are classified; a program is worked
out by mutual agreement. Every inmate starts off with
a job, he is then placed in a school situation . . .
If they earn it, they go to the pre-release center and
then they are released to the community and
voluntarily can be in after-care followup for four
months."

Perhaps one of the most prolific, yet simple, statements
concerning the national issue of the effectiveness of treatment
programs for offenders was stated by Jay Ashe, Deputy
Superintendent of Human Services:

The thing that aggravates me when I hear about
rehabilitation, which is a bad word, it doesn't work,
is that human services have no focus in the
correctional system. They are trimming on the
trees. I walk into a correctional system and they
(treatment staff) are way over here someplace. And
then some commissioner is saying they don't work.
They don't have any focus. Here they do — they have
a priority.

Management Style

Perhaps the best description of management at the jail is
professionalism. That is, after major decisions are made by the
sheriff and his two deputy administrators, the rest of the staff,
especially human services personnel, are expected to carry out
their objectives by utilizing their skills and ideas in a
professional manner. They present program ideas, implementation
strategies, write grants for funding and operate their own
programs so that they are well integrated with the overall goals
of the institution. All human services staff appear to work with
a great deal of independence, yet communicate with each other both
formally through meetings and informally throughout the day.
Everyone seems to know what others are doing and very few
organizational conflicts appear to exist between personnel working
in the numerous programs. One canot help but notice the
enthusiasm of the staff when describing the programs which they
manage or work in.

Conclusions

Our description and analysis of the Hampden County Jail should hopefully provide other sheriffs and jail administrators with practical insights about the maintenance of inmate programs and facility renovation in a county that is experiencing budget restraints.

The following summary indicates those factors which have been significant in enabling county corrections to maintain programs, receive funds for jail renovation projects, and meet the requirements of national jail standards:

1. The continual effort to maintain close political association with county commissioners, county advisory boards, and the state legislative committee on counties.

2. Planning for alternative sources of funding for the jail as federal funds become depleted.

3. Constant use of the local media, radio, television, and newspapers for the purpose of informing the public of the programs and goals of the corrections program as well as identifying problems which could impede program efforts for inmates.

4. Maintaining an open door policy to community groups and political officials in order for them to be knowledgeable of the work the jail staff is doing and the need for political support for the necessary funds to accomplish overall program goals.

5. Planning an implementing inmate reintegration programs with a counterpart in the community in order to provide employment and ongoing services for released prisoners once returned to the community.

6. Utilization of city and county public agencies for the benefit of prisoners, especially in the areas of job training skills for inmates.

7. Maintaing a high profile with the political machinery of the county and state.

8. Consistently searching for new sources of funding and attempting to get industry and labor involved in the corrections program for the purpose of attaining financial appropriations and further community support for the institution's goals.

9. Implementing an advisory board comprised of members from the professional and business community to provide expert advise on the overall jail program, as well as to provide a vital link to the private sector.

10. Maintaining a balance between security and human services which has resulted in both programs working harmoniously.

11. Hiring professional personnel who are given a wide latitude to express new program ideas and are responsible in getting these programs inplemented with support from the top administrators.

12. The sheriff's role as one which primarily consists of external politics in gaining needed financial resources for the jail and letting the two deputy administrators share the bulk of the responsiblity for the daily operation of the facility.

13. Viewing the attainment of national jail standards as a high priority.

14. Close association with other sheriffs in the state to form a coalition to attempt to attain necessary funding for jails from the state legislature.

15. Political associations at the state level for the purpose of becoming appointed to criminal justice groups that make recommendations and dispurse federal funds.

16. Providing the state department of corrections with reciprocal solutions for keeping a number of state inmates in the county jail while receiving state reimbursement for having them serve their sentence there.

17. Utilizing volunteers to work with inmates in various human services programs at very little cost to the county.

18. Keeping abreast of the situation in corrections at the national level and being knowledgeable of programs that appear to be worthwhile in other facilities.

19. Planning for physical plant renovations and gaining support for such projects at the county and state level of government.

20. Prioritizing human service programs as the major objective for the operation of the jail, thus constantly developing strategies to maintain such services.

Hampden County will be facing even more severe budget constraints in the next few years. This will present Sheriff Ashe and his staff with their most difficult challenge to date. The issue of maintaining programs will be based in large part in the sheriff's ability to utilize the necessary community and political support for funding that he has already developed. Because of the sheriff and his two top administrators' long-term use of developing managerial strategies internal to the organization and externally gaining support groups in the community, it appears that the Hampden County correctional operation will not suffer the degree of restraints of diminishing resource allocations that other facilities within the state may. A big test, which will measure the sheriff's political capabilities on the state level, will be the outcome of his attempts to attain the four million dollars for jail renovation projects potentially funded by the state to the county.

Mark Pogrebin is a Professor of Criminal Justice and Public Affairs at the University of Colorado at Denver. He is coauthor of <u>The Invisible Justice System: Discretion and the Law</u>, and has a new anthology forthcoming entitled <u>Police Administrative Issues</u>. Currently he is on Fellowship with the National Institute of Corrections conducting a national study of jail correction's officers.